Lectionary Tales For The Pulpit

Series IV
Cycle A

Gregory L. Tolle

CSS Publishing Company, Inc., Lima, Ohio

LECTIONARY TALES FOR THE PULPIT, SERIES IV, CYCLE A

Library of Congress Cataloging-in-Publication Data

Tolle, Gregory L., 1966-
Lectionary tales for the pulpit. Series IV, cycle A / Gregory L. Tolle.
p. cm.
ISBN 0-7880-2320-9 (perfect bound : alk. paper)
1. Lectionary preaching. 2. Bible—Homiletical use. I. Title.

BV4211.3.T65 2004
251—dc22

2004013761

For more information about CSS Publishing Company resources, visit our website at www.csspub.com or e-mail us at custserv@csspub.com or call (800) 241-4056.

ISBN 0-7880-2320-9 PRINTED IN U.S.A.

I dedicate these stories in the wonderful memory of my mother, Joan Tolle. I regret that she did not live long enough to see this book completed. I believe, by the grace of God and in the mystery of the faith that she knows of her youngest son's accomplishment. I also dedicate this book to my father, Leonard Tolle, who like my mother, made so many sacrifices to give me greater opportunities than he had in life. I'm so grateful for your love and guidance.

Table Of Contents

Introduction

I once had a man who decided to leave the church at which I was the minister. He told someone else within the church that he didn't like my sermons. (I know that his words are hardly an endorsement for this book, but bear with me.) In particular, he thought I used too many illustrations. He apparently wanted preaching that included more theological lecture. Based on the new church where he chose to worship, he also wanted more judgment and less grace in the sermons he heard.

After hearing the man's comments on my use of illustrations, I responded by saying, "I guess he doesn't like how Jesus preached. Christ's preaching and teaching was filled with stories. He taught in parables because he knew that people could relate to them. His stories spoke a truth."

I regret that this man did not understand the importance of stories to illustrate divine truth. From experience, I know people do not always remember specific points in a sermon, unless they attach it to a story. I remember stories my father preached 25 years ago. My wife has repeated stories preached by our minister ten years ago. Obviously, we are still hearing and discussing the stories Jesus told more than 2,000 years ago. Stories have an incredible power. I hope the stories in this book relay the power to move people to a greater faith.

Advent 1
Isaiah 2:1-5

Yule Shoppers Clash

He shall judge between the nations, and shall arbitrate for many peoples; they shall beat their swords into plowshares, and their spears into pruning hooks; nation shall not lift up sword against nation, neither shall they learn war any more. (v. 4)

It was Thanksgiving weekend — the beginning of the official Christmas shopping season. Television networks had started showing the "Peace on earth, good will toward men" movies like *It's a Wonderful Life* and *A Christmas Carol*. However, the Saturday newspaper reported on the real events of the Friday following Thanksgiving. The headline read "Yule Shoppers Clash."

The first line of the article read, " 'Keep the Peace' replaced 'Peace on Earth' as the holiday season's official greeting Friday when spirited arguments broke out at two Tulsa stores on perhaps the most-frenzied shopping day of the year."

The Tulsa police had to stop two separate fights — one at a Target and one at a Best Buy. What caused the mini riots? Arguments over a place in line to enter the stores. Shoppers arrived early to claim the place to be one of the first to enter the stores. The stores were offering special promotions to a specific number of first customers. These shoppers were facing assault and battery charges over free Beanie Babies and Hot Wheels.

With a poetic promise of peace from Isaiah, we wonder when it will be realized. During the season in which we find ourselves with a wonderful giving spirit, we still see people picking up swords and spears. One must remember that the Hebrew word for peace is *shalom*, and it means wholeness or well-being. In *Wishful Thinking: A Seeker's ABC*, Frederick Buechner defines shalom as "having everything you need to be wholly and happily yourself."

To experience peace as we prepare for the Prince of Peace is to love one another. We have peace when we realize we have love. It is then that we lay down swords and spears and Beanie Babies and Hot Wheels. Isaiah invites us to participate in this peace.

(Details taken from an 11/28/98 story from the *Tulsa World*.)

Advent 2
Matthew 3:1-12

The Fire Within

"I baptize you with water for repentance, but one who is more powerful than I is coming after me; I am not worthy to carry his sandals. He will baptize you with the Holy Spirit and fire." (v. 11)

In 1989, I was the youth minister of Grand Avenue United Methodist Church in McAlester, Oklamona. I also assisted in leading worship, including reading scripture in our Christmas Eve Candlelight Service. As I was driving to the church for the service that year, I saw a disturbing sight near the church while I was about two blocks away. The church sat up on a hill, so I had a clear view of two bright red fire trucks parked on the street just east of the building. My heart sunk as my eyes widened. The Presbyterian Church was immediately north of our church. I know it was wrong and shallow, but after seeing those trucks I offered a quick prayer: "Please, Lord, let it be the Presbyterians. Let it be the Presbyterians."

As I pulled in the parking lot, I soon discovered it was not the Presbyterians. The fire was at Grand Avenue UMC, a stately four-story brick building built in the 1920s. Christmas Eve fell on a Sunday that year and apparently a children's Sunday school class didn't blow out the candles on their Advent wreath after their lesson that morning. Fortunately, they did close the door to the classroom before they left, so the fire was contained to the one classroom. Later as choir members arrived for a quick rehearsal, some of their children ventured to the third floor and discovered smoke leaking out from under the door. They very wisely didn't open the door, or the fire would have spread instantaneously. Instead they told their parents who called the fire station.

By the time I arrived, the fire was out, but there was still the issue of the Christmas Eve Candlelight Service. Because the sanctuary was adjacent to the classroom, there was too much smoke damage for the room to be utilized for a worship service. Very quickly, we began setting up chairs in the fellowship hall to hold our service. The firemen were not gone long before we started the service. One of the inspirational moments of our service every year was ending the hour by singing "Silent Night" while everyone holds a lighted candle. It was an interesting feeling that year to hold a candle knowing the fire we held in our hand had almost destroyed our church building. It was eerie, but at the same time, it also created a real sense of gratitude for what we had. We could have lost the building, but we didn't. More importantly, we could have canceled the service, but we didn't. Instead of creating chaos, the fire had pulled the congregation together in a new way that forced us to focus on God instead of possessions.

We generally think of fire for its destructive capabilities, but it also has a positive strength. John the Baptist extolled that Jesus would baptize with fire. That baptizing fire would create a new being. The fire that chased us out of the sanctuary created a way for all the worshipers to leave as changed people. Our hearts were warmed in a unique way that evening as the Christmas story was retold. As we left after the service, we left with a new understanding of being the light of Christ for the world. I believe that we left with a new fire within.

Advent 3
Matthew 11:2-11

Why Come To Earth?

When John heard in prison what the Messiah was doing, he sent word by his disciples and said to him, "Are you the one who is to come, or are we to wait for another?" Jesus answered them, "Go and tell John what you hear and see: the blind receive their sight, the lame walk, the lepers are cleansed, the deaf hear, the dead are raised, and the poor have good news brought to them." (vv. 2-5)

There was once a man who didn't believe in God, and he was quick to let others know his opinion. However, his wife was a Christian who raised their children with her beliefs. She encouraged them to ignore their father's critical comments.

One snowy Christmas Eve as his wife was leaving their farm to take their children to a Christmas Eve service, she asked him to come. He refused, saying, "Christmas is nonsense! What kind of God comes to earth as a man? What unrealistic humility. It's ridiculous!" So she and the children left, and he stayed home.

A little while later, the howling winds called him to look outside. The gentle snow was turning into a blizzard. The thickness of the snow made it hard to see. He returned to his chair to relax by the crackling fire. Then he heard a loud thump. Something had hit the window. Then another thump. He looked out the window, but couldn't see anything in the blinding snow. So he put on his heavy coat and ventured outside to see what was making the noise.

Several yards from his house he saw a flock of wild geese flapping and aimlessly confused. Apparently they had been flying south for the winter when they got caught in the snowstorm. They were stranded on his farm looking for food and shelter. Evidently, a couple of them had been attracted to the light from his window.

The man felt sorry for the geese and wanted to help them. The barn would be a great place for them. It was warm and safe. Surely they would be able to continue their journey the next day. So he walked over to the barn and opened the doors wide. He hoped the geese would notice the open barn and go inside. He waited, but the geese just fluttered around aimlessly. They didn't even seem to notice the barn let alone realize the safety available.

Then the man tried to shoo them into the barn, but that just seemed to scare them, and they moved further away. He went into the house and returned with breadcrumbs to make a trail leading to the barn. They still didn't catch on. He was getting frustrated as all his attempts to help were failing. Nothing he did could get them to go into the barn where they would be warm and safe.

He exclaimed, "Why don't they follow me? Can't they see this is the only place where they can survive the storm?" He deliberated for a moment and realized that these wild geese would never follow a human. He thought to himself, "If only I were a goose, then I could save them."

Then he had an idea. He went into the barn, got one of his own geese, and carried it in his arms as he circled around behind the flock of wild geese. He then released it. His goose flew through the flock and straight into the barn and one by one the other geese followed it to safety.

He stood silently for a moment as the words he had spoken a few minutes earlier replayed in his mind: "If only I were a goose, then I could save them!" Then he thought about what he had said to his wife earlier. "Why would God want to be like us? That's ridiculous!"

Suddenly it all made sense. That is what God had done. We were like the geese — blind, lost, and perishing. God became human to show us the way to salvation. The man realized the meaning of Christmas. He stood in the midst of the storm with an unusual peace. He knew why Jesus was born. He fell to his knees in the snow, and prayed his first prayer: "Thank you, God, for coming in human form to get me out of the storm!"

Advent 4
Matthew 1:18-25

The Perfect Imperfect Pageant

When Joseph awoke from sleep, he did as the angel of the Lord commanded him; he took her as his wife, but had no marital relations with her until she had borne a son; and he named him Jesus. (vv. 24-25)

In *The Good News From North Haven*, Michael Lindvall tells of how a Christmas pageant gone awry shows the great love and commitment that Joseph had for God and Mary. For 46 years Alvina Johnson had directed the pageant of his church, Second Presbyterian Church in North Haven, Minnesota. And for 46 years, the Christmas play remained unchanged. She strove for perfection, which meant she made simplicity a priority. As such, she only allowed nine parts, which excluded several children of the church. She also was a stickler for tradition, which meant the play was a recitation of the King James Version of the Christmas story from Luke chapter 2.

But after 46 years several of the young mothers sought a change. They felt more children should be allowed to participate. So some of the mothers held a *coup d'etat* and took over the pageant. However, with the change in leadership came less than perfect results. More sheep meant more problems — especially when these rural children knew how unruly sheep behave.

The imperfection culminated at the pageant when Mary and Joseph entered. Now Mary was wonderful. She gently held a baby doll in a blue blanket. She peered into the face of the doll with eyes that appeared to really see the infant Christ. But Joseph was another story. He had largely gotten the part because Alvina Johnson had rejected him from the Christmas Pageant more times than any other kid in church.

The plan was for Mary and Joseph to walk in as the Narrator read from the traditional King James text, "And Joseph also went up from Galilee, out of the city of Nazareth, into Judea, unto the city of David, which is called Bethlehem, (because he was of the house and lineage of David:) To be taxed with Mary his espoused wife, being great with child."

This was the plan. This is what the Narrator had practiced for months. But a few hours before the performance, one of the new young leaders had observed that the children struggled with the King James English. As the young mothers discussed the problem, they asked, "What kid knows what 'great with child' means?" In their revolutionary fervor, they decided to switch to the Good News translation of the Bible. After all, it would make the story more understandable for everyone.

So during the performance when Mary and Joseph entered, the Narrator read, "Joseph went to register with Mary who was promised in marriage to him. She was pregnant." The word *pregnant* seemed to echo through the PA system. Poor little Joseph stopped in his tracks. He gave Mary an astounded look, and then looked out at the congregation and said, "Pregnant? What do you mean, pregnant?"

The congregation burst out laughing. Lindvall's wife laughed so hard she cried. She wiped the tears from her eyes and leaned over to him and said, "You know, that may well be just what Joseph actually said." The pageant may not have been perfect, but the imperfection better displayed the character of Joseph as he followed God's command to stay with Mary and raise the Son of God.

Christmas Eve
Luke 2:1-14 (15-20)

Silent Night, Holy Night

But the angel said to them, "Do not be afraid; for see — I am bringing you good news of a great joy for all the people: to you is born this day in the city of David a Savior, who is the Messiah, the Lord." (vv. 10-11)

It is funny how we begin to see a series of coincidences for what they often are — providence. God has a way of stringing together the unlikely as a sign. For instance, look at the history of the hymn "Silent Night" and my occasion to read it. The story of its creation is worth repeating. In 1818, Joseph Mohr was a 26-year-old assistant priest at St. Nicholas' Church at Oberndorf, a village in the Austrian Alps. In the days before Christmas, the old church organ was out of commission. Legend says mice had chewed through the bellows. It would be spring before the itinerant organ repairman would be in the area to fix it. This created the obvious problem that there would be no organ accompaniment for Christmas Eve Mass.

To help remedy this, Mohr approached 31-year-old Franz X. Gruber, the organist at St. Nicholas' Church and a schoolteacher in the neighboring village of Arnsdorf. Two years prior, when Mohr was assigned to a small church in Mariapfarr, he wrote a poem depicting the birth of Christ. Mohr asked Gruber to set the poem to music so that they could sing it together with guitar accompaniment at the midnight service. They named their composition "Song From Heaven," and unveiled it December 24, 1818. Since then, it has become the classic carol we know as "Silent Night." It has been translated into virtually every language and has become a staple at Christmas Eve candlelight services around the world.

Yet, Mohr and Gruber never realized how popular their little song would become. Since "Silent Night" was written as a stop-gap when the organ quit, the pair didn't plan on the song being sung after the initial performance in 1818. In fact, the two men parted ways shortly after Christmas as Mohr was transferred away from Oberndorf. The song's popularity was localized and then soon forgotten.

However, in 1825, Karl Mauracher was hired to rebuild the organ at the St. Nicholas' church. After making the repairs, Mauracher asked Gruber to play the organ to check the tuning. Gruber played "Song From Heaven." Mauracher loved the song and requested permission to take the song back home with him to the Ziller Valley in the mountains of Tyrol. Permission was granted and Mauracher took a handwritten copy of the words and musical notation of "Song From Heaven." The Ziller Valley was home to folk choirs who performed for wealthy noblemen all over Europe. One of these singing groups was a quartet of children — Caroline, Joseph, Andreas, and Amalie Strasser. They spread "Silent Night" wherever they went. They performed at the Royal Saxon Court Chapel of Piessenburg Castle in Leipzig and the Royal Court of Berlin in Prussia. However without copyright laws, no credit was ever given to the composers and the song became associated with the Ziller Valley folk choirs. The song commonly became known as "The Tyrolean Folk Carol."

It is a miracle that Mohr and Gruber were ever credited for their work. Over the years, the carol had been attributed to many different composers including Herr Hadyn, Franz Joseph Haydn, Mozart, and Beethoven. Fortunately in 1854, the director of the Royal Court Choir of Berlin began to research the origins of the carol because it was the favorite Christmas hymn of King Friedrich Wilhelm IV of Prussia. The director was a curious academic, who traced the true origins of the carol to Salzburg where Mohr had first written the poem in 1816. If not for this disciplined research, we might never have recognized Joseph Mohr and Franz X. Gruber as the composers of "Silent Night."

This research was confirmed in 1997 when a volunteer at the Carolino Augusteum Museum in Salzburg, Austria, discovered an original handwritten Mohr manuscript. Handwriting experts dated the manuscript to 1820, making it the oldest known manuscript of "Silent Night." The lower left hand corner bears the signature of Josef Mohr, followed by "1816" designating the year the original poem was written. The upper right-hand corner designates Gruber as the tune's composer with the words "Melodie von Fr. Xav. Gruber." This silences any doubts about who wrote the music for this world-famous carol.

Many of the circumstances surrounding this story could be termed coincidences. It was a coincidence that the organ didn't work precipitating the need for a new song played on guitar. It was a coincidence that the song was discovered and circulated by an organ repairman who happened to be from an area that sang all over Europe. It was a coincidence that the carol was a favorite of the Prussian king so that the choir director would research the history discovering Mohr and Gruber as the composers. And it was coincidence that the 1820 manuscript was uncovered which confirmed the authenticity of the composers. But when looking through the eyes of faith, we often see that coincidences are, in fact, God's intervention.

I believe God intervened when Bill Warner came to visit me a couple days after I read the history of "Silent Night." Bill, a Catholic, is the widower of one of my members. He stopped by the office bringing a four-foot high wooden crucifix for me to see. The crucifix was carved out of apple wood by Bill's great-grandfather. Jesus was depicted in great detail as attention was given to his hair, teeth, fingernails, and an expression of agony. Bill also brought a newspaper article protected in a glassed-in frame. The newspaper article was from a Fort Smith, Arkansas, newspaper dated December 24, 1967. The article showed pictures of the large crucifix and told how it had been passed through the family eventually to Bill's mother.

The article also shared the story of Bill's talented great-grandfather who was skilled in more than just woodcarving. He was also a very talented organ craftsman who lived in the Ziller Valley of Austria in 1825. Bill's great-grandfather is Karl Mauracher, the man who spread "Silent Night" throughout the world.

Was it a coincidence that I read the "Silent Night" story a few days before Bill's visit with me? No, of course not. It was the unfolding of a God story. It was a gentle reminder that God is in our midst. Which, not so incidentally, is what Christmas is all about. We celebrate the birth of our Savior and Messiah.

Christmas 1
Hebrews 2:10-18

Identifying With Suffering

For it is clear that he did not come to help angels, but the descendants of Abraham. Therefore he had to become like his brothers and sisters in every respect, so that he might be a merciful and faithful high priest in the service of God, to make a sacrifice of atonement for the sins of the people. Because he himself was tested by what he suffered, he is able to help those who are being tested. (vv. 16-18)

In the book *Walking Taylor Home*, Brian Schrauger tells of his son, Taylor. The boy was eight years old when he began to feel periodic aches in his legs. It seemed like normal growing pains at first. But then the soreness turned into a limp. A month before his tenth birthday, Taylor went to an orthopedic clinic. An MRI revealed that he had a melon-sized tumor growing near his inner pelvis. A biopsy revealed osteo-sarcoma, a vicious cancer that grows from the bone. The mass becomes hard and has a stabbing effect.

Taylor began being treated with chemotherapy. Two days after his tenth birthday, he discovered that he could pull out his hair. He yelled to his dad to watch because he thought it was cool. Brian admonished Taylor to stop pulling out his hair because he was only making his bald spot bigger. However, Brian knew that he could not stop Taylor from losing his hair. It is an inevitable side effect of the chemo.

He suggested to Taylor that he buzz it down to a stubble and make the bald spot less noticeable. Off to the garage they went with electric clippers. Taylor's mom took pictures during the haircut. They laughed and played as they left a momentary Mohawk.

They also left one tuft, which was tied with a ribbon. They gathered his blond hair in a Ziploc bag.

A week later, even the stubble had fallen out. Taylor now had a chrome dome. Brian felt so terrible for his son that he snuck into the bathroom one afternoon and trimmed his gray hair to stubble. He lathered up and shaved off the stubble.

Brian joined Taylor at dinner to show off his cue ball look. Taylor grinned and said, "Feels kinda weird, doesn't it?" Brian agreed. But they took a positive approach to the change. In a take-off of the movie *Men in Black*, they became Men in Baldness.

A few months later, the tumor was removed and Taylor's left leg was amputated. A year later, the Schraugers discovered that the cancer had spread to Taylor's lungs and pelvic sphere. A quarter of his left lung was removed. The cancer continued to worsen over the next five months, so in desperation the doctors tried radiation therapy even though osteo-sarcomas are highly resistant to it. The radiation was not effective, and Taylor died twelve days shy of his twelfth birthday.

In an e-mail to loved ones, Brian wrote, "As his body declined, his spirit shined brighter and brighter. It was so brilliant, everyone who saw it was stunned." No doubt, Taylor's faith was impacted by the way his father lived out his faith. Like Christ who took a human form to identify with our suffering, Brian shaved his head to identify with Taylor's suffering — both the disease and the chemo. Brian sacrificed to show his love to his son, just as Christ sacrificed to show his love for the world.

Christmas 2
Ephesians 1:3-14

Welcome To The Family

He destined us for adoption as his children through Jesus Christ, according to the good pleasure of his will, to the praise of his glorious grace that he freely bestowed on us in the Beloved. (vv. 5-6)

Mike and Wendy DeMoss walked down the aisle for the first time as husband and wife. Of course they were elated. After months of planning, they were finally married. All that was left was celebrating with their friends and family who had gathered to join in their celebration. They stepped outside the church with the rest of the wedding party behind them.

A few moments later all of the guests made their way out. Friends and family were eager to greet the young newlyweds. They all flocked to them to offer words of joy and congratulations. Wendy's grandmother, Velma, exited the church. She looked diligently for the tall and handsome groom with dark hair and a cheerful smile. She wanted to meet the man who had made her granddaughter so happy. She located young Mr. DeMoss and went directly to him. Her arms were outstretched as she approached him. Then she threw her arms around him with a warm grandmotherly hug, and said, "Welcome to the family!"

The young man was shocked. See, she hadn't hugged the young groom and welcomed him into the family. She had hugged and welcomed Mike's twin brother. He thought he was merely attending his brother's wedding and he gets adopted into the family. Even though he insisted he was not the new family member, he had been accepted into Velma's family circle anyway. The fact that he wasn't the groom was irrelevant. As far as Velma was concerned, once you're in, you're in forever. She was not going to exclude her new grandson's brother from the family just because of a mistaken identity.

Of course, Mike's brother had no claim on the family. He wasn't born into it and didn't even marry into it. But he was loved into it. That's how God works with us. We have no claim on the faith family, and yet, God adopts us anyway. God's grace comes to us through Christ and brings us into the family. Loving arms are wrapped around us, and a voice says, "Welcome to the family!"

The Epiphany Of Our Lord
Matthew 2:1-12

Out Of The Minds Of Babes

When they saw that the star had stopped, they were overwhelmed with joy. On entering the house, they saw the child with Mary his mother; and they knelt down and paid him homage. Then, opening their treasure chests, they offered him gifts of gold, frankincense, and myrrh. (vv. 10-11)

We can learn so much from children. A few years back, my son, Spencer, turned four about a month before Christmas. He decided one day to rearrange the figures from our nativity. When my wife, Hadley, set them up, they were carefully placed in a row — organized, balanced, and placed to perfection. Spencer, on the other hand, decided they should be huddled in a tight circle around the Baby Jesus. Hadley discovered the change and pointed it out to me. I responded, "You know, that's probably more accurate. They would squeeze in close to see the Christ child." Ah, the wisdom of a child's view.

Spencer knew that when you're excited about something, you jump right in. The scripture says the Wise Men "were overwhelmed with joy" and that "they knelt down and paid him homage." If they were filled with joyous worship, they wouldn't line up like they were taking a family picture. They would get as close a possible to the Christ child.

Children experience the joy of Christmas like no others. It's instinctive. On December 25, adults can manage to act like children with awe and wonder. But what about Epiphany? After Christmas Day has passed and all the presents have been opened, are the thrills and wonder gone? What excites us other than the after-Christmas sales and college football bowl games? Is the only surprise we expect attached to the overwhelming shock of the looming credit card bill?

But what if you viewed Christmas through new eyes — the eyes of a child. Ever notice that children are still excited way after Christmas? Why is that? Because they are still overjoyed with new toys, visiting relatives, and Christmas treats. Like the Wise Men, we have been given a wonderful gift. That gift is worthy of our praise not just on December 25, and not just Epiphany, but all year long.

Just because we are used to seeing the nativity scene in a straight line, it doesn't mean it has to be that way. We can see through the eyes of a child. And just because the norm is to pack Christmas up and store it in the attic, doesn't mean we can't return to our lives as renewed people who have been inspired by a precious gift. We can allow the gift of the birth of a savior to change us for more than a day. Spencer's nativity arrangement reminded me of that. We enter the kingdom as little children filled with awe, joy, and wonder — overwhelmed that Someone cared enough to give us a priceless gift. Christmas is not just an ordinary holiday that passes on one day. It is an opportunity for an entire lifetime of joyous transformation.

The Baptism Of Our Lord / Epiphany 1 / Ordinary Time 1
Matthew 3:13-17

Been Baptized

> *And when Jesus had been baptized, just as he came up from the water, suddenly the heavens were opened to him and he saw the Spirit of God descending like a dove and alighting on him. And a voice from heaven said, "This is my Son, the Beloved, with whom I am well pleased."* (vv. 16-17)

A pastor moved to a new community and was ready to get started in ministry there. One of his members came by one morning and asked if he could give the pastor a tour of the community. The pastor jumped at the chance. They loaded up in the man's pickup and began the tour.

Soon after they had started, the man pulled up to a four-way stop. Most small rural towns have one of these intersections. It is the hub of the town. There is a bar on one corner, the bank is on another, a convenience store is on the third, and the fourth is an empty building or a vacant lot. As the man stopped the truck, he gently placed his thumb on his forehead and whispered, "Been baptized."

Several blocks up the street, he pulled over at an old house and invited the preacher to join him. The two went to the door and knocked several times. Finally they heard, "Hold on, I am on my way." A kind-looking elderly woman answered the door. She gave the driver a great big hug and a smile. The man told the preacher to reach out and shake hands with a "saint." The kind lady firmly gripped the preacher's hand as the man once again touched his forehead and whispered, "Been baptized."

After a good visit, the two men left. The tour came to an end when the driver asked the preacher if he would like a soft drink.

They pulled up to the convenience store. No sooner had they gotten out of the truck, than another man approached the driver, wagging a finger in his face and complaining about community problems. His voice grew louder as his anger became a driving force. The preacher's new friend responded by simply placing his thumb on his forehead and mumbling under his breath, "Been baptized."

They bought a couple of soft drinks and returned to the church. Before the preacher left the truck, he said, "I hate to pry, but I have to ask. I noticed that several times today you touched your forehead and mumbled under your breath. Why?"

The driver smiled, and put his arm around the preacher. He explained, "You see, it has been several years since I have come to know and love God. It took me a while to understand how much God loves and forgives me. A few years ago, I went before the church and asked that they forgive me and accept me into their family. The next day, I went around and told all my friends, and even my enemies, that I was now a Christian — that my old life was gone and I was going to serve God in all I did.

"I touched my forehead and mumbled the words 'been baptized' at the four-way stop because the bar was my church before I became a Christian. The bank was where all my work and effort went before I realized that working for God was more important.

"I did the same when we stopped at the lady's house because she was the first person to welcome me into the family of faith. She hugged me and told me that not only did God love me, but also the whole faith community loved me and forgave me. I was a part of the family of God.

"And lastly, I did the same thing when that man confronted me at the store because it reminded me of who I really am. I am a child of God. Loved, forgiven, and accepted. My old ways are gone. My old self is dead. I must, therefore, watch and try to be Christ-like in all that I do. I know now that this is the way to live out my call."

Sometimes we need to remember that we have been baptized and that through baptism, we have been claimed by God. We share in Christ's baptism, and are called sons and daughters of God. Just as the Spirit of God descended on Jesus as his baptism, the Spirit comes to us to transform us with love and forgiveness.

Epiphany 2 / Ordinary Time 2
John 1:29-42

Old Times

When Jesus turned and saw them following, he said to them, "What are you looking for?" They said to him, "Rabbi" (which translated means Teacher), "where are you staying?" He said to them, "Come and see." They came and saw where he was staying, and they remained with him that day. It was about four o'clock in the afternoon. One of the two who heard John speak and followed him was Andrew, Simon Peter's brother. He first found his brother Simon and said to him, "We have found the Messiah" (which is translated Anointed). (vv. 38-41)

After church one Sunday, my family and I had lunch with an old friend. For nearly four years we had lived twenty miles apart, but had rarely seen each other. I call Marie my friend, but that really doesn't describe the relationship. When I was between the ages of five and nine, she was my babysitter and second mother. She was Mrs. Reece back then. Her only child had graduated and moved off to college. She had a strong love for little children.

When I was a kid, I loved going to Mrs. Reece's house. She had a basement filled with toys waiting to be explored. There was a drawer beneath a window seat in the dining room that also had toys and games. There were stairs leading to the second floor that also became my playground. I would jump from the first step to the floor and then move up one step and jump again. This continued until I got hurt or too scared to go any higher. I also liked to sit on the steps and scoot down step by step.

But as neat as the house and toys were, the best thing about going to Mrs. Reece's house was Mrs. Reece. She loved children and as a child, you sensed that. I don't know why she didn't have more children, but she should have. She had the love to give. But I guess it didn't matter, she found more children to love. I was fortunate to be one of them.

On that Sunday afternoon 24 years later, I had lunch with Mrs. Reece. She still loved children and my three-year-old son, Spencer, had discovered this. Maybe it's osmosis. Even though he had never been to her house and didn't really know her, he overcame his normal initial shyness displayed at new places and around new people. He immediately explored the house and acted as if everything was normal procedure. We had an outstanding home-cooked meal and a lovely conversation. Finally it was time to leave, but before we left, Mrs. Reece joked to Spencer about staying and spending the night. After knowing her for two hours, he accepted her invitation without hesitation. As I've said, Mrs. Reece has a way with children.

My wife and I discussed this on the drive back home. I mentioned Mrs. Reece's demeanor as the reason Spencer would accept her so readily. As parents, we've noticed several adults who try to force themselves on children. They are generally nice people, but they haven't allowed enough time for our kids to develop a rapport with them. Mrs. Reece has a way of being inviting to children without being pushy. She pointed out the toys and then went about her business. She first let Spencer come to her instead of fawning all over him. She asked a couple of simple questions that are important to a three-year-old. Spencer felt comfortable, and consequently, he responded well to her.

During this discussion, it became apparent to me that we could learn a lot from Mrs. Reece about sharing our faith. All too often, generally nice people with good intentions get too pushy with their faith. We don't wait to develop a comfortable rapport. Or we get so uptight about sharing our faith that our discomfort becomes discomforting. As Christians, we need to be inviting and friendly — engaging people when they feel comfortable. When people feel comfortable, they will respond. Jesus' invitation to John's disciples was a simple, "Come and see." Andrew's invitation to his brother Simon was much the same. Neither invitation was heavy-handed — just like Mrs. Reece.

Epiphany 3 / Ordinary Time 3
Matthew 4:12-23

Don't Hang Up When The Call Comes

As he walked by the Sea of Galilee, he saw two brothers, Simon, who is called Peter, and Andrew his brother, casting a net into the sea — for they were fishermen. And he said to them, "Follow me, and I will make you fish for people." Immediately they left their nets and followed him. As he went from there, he saw two other brothers, James son of Zebedee and his brother John, in the boat with their father Zebedee, mending their nets, and he called them. Immediately they left the boat and their father, and followed him. (vv. 18-22)

It came during finals week of my freshman year spring semester. The Call. Most of my finals were on Monday, Tuesday, and Wednesday, but my last final of my freshman year was on Friday. That meant I had all day Thursday to study, which I did. However too much studying can fry your brain, so I gave myself Thursday evening off to relax. My friend Dean worked in the dorm as an R.A. — a Resident Assistant. Even though he was finished with his finals, he couldn't start his summer vacation until everyone checked out of the dorm. So that Thursday evening, Dean and I watched a movie in his room. However, during the movie, I struggled to stay awake. The movie was interesting enough, but I guess studying all day had taken its toll. So, after the movie I went straight to my room to go to bed.

My room was basically empty. My roommate had already moved out, and I had packed up all nonessential belongings. I quickly went through my nightly hygiene routine and slipped into bed. But, I couldn't sleep. After fighting sleep during the movie, I was now wide-awake. As I lay in bed, I had one thought repeating itself over and over in my mind. No matter what I tried, I couldn't rid myself of this atrocious thought: Greg, you should be a minister like your father.

These were not words I wanted to hear. In the first place, I had a test the next morning. The only thing I needed in my head was correct test answers. Secondly, I did not, under any circumstances, want to be a minister. I was a Mass Communications major. I was following the money trail into advertising. Church was a nice place to visit, but I didn't want to work there. I had lived the life of a preacher's kid, why would I want to live the life of the preacher? I knew what it was like to be a minister — low pay, long hours, and some of the people aren't always nice.

So after a two-hour struggle with this thought, I did what many of the people in the Bible did — I made a deal with God. I said, "God, if this is you, and you really want me to be a minister, let me get some sleep so I can take my test tomorrow. Then, we can talk about this afterwards." I fell asleep nearly instantaneously.

After taking my test, I avoided dealing with the call. A friend was getting married the next day so I left town for the nuptials. After the wedding, I spent the night in town and went to church the next morning, which was Sunday. While in worship, I decided to test God. It was not without biblical precedent — Gideon among others had tested God. It was not that I was incredibly biblically literate, but it was more human instinct and skepticism. I remembered many people telling my dad how they felt he had preached a sermon directly to them. So I challenged God to have the minister address my alleged call to ministry. God obliged. As an illustration that morning, the minister told the story of how he had struggled when he had been called to ministry!

God - 1. Greg - 0.

But it was still not proof enough for me. The Sunday the following week, I was visiting another congregation in another town. Hoping the occurrence of the previous Sunday was a mere coincidence, I proposed once again that the minister should preach directly to me on the issue of this alleged call to ministry. The minister's sermon topic was "giftedness" — how God has given each of us a gift that should in turn be used for ministry.

Now, understand that I was voted Most Talented my senior year in high school. This was largely due to my involvement in competitive speech. I competed in the state competition as a senior. I had never preached a sermon in my life to that point, but there was no debating that public speaking was an area in which I had gifts. I was not a learned preacher, but I was an accomplished public speaker.

God - 2. Greg still 0.

Still not convinced, I continued an internal struggle over the next few weeks. Eventually though, I gave in to the call and shared the experience with my family. The moment I shared my call, I felt a real joy and an overwhelming sense of relief. It was as if a burden was lifted from me, and I knew that my call was real. I was given a sense of peace that words cannot explain. I knew that God was real.

Simon, Andrew, James, and John must have sensed that peace so clearly for they followed immediately. They didn't try to bargain their way out or convince themselves of coincidences. They simply followed when the master called them. And what an incredible journey it turned out to be!

WWJD

> *"With what shall I come before the LORD, and bow myself before God on high? Shall I come before him with burnt offerings, with calves a year old? Will the LORD be pleased with thousands of rams, with ten thousands of rivers of oil? Shall I give my firstborn for my transgression, the fruit of my body for the sin of my soul?" He has told you, O mortal, what is good; and what does the LORD require of you but to do justice, and to love kindness, and to walk humbly with your God? (vv. 6-8)*

On March 5, 1986, I was a student at Oklahoma City University. That evening on the other side of the city, Vonda and Paul Bellofatta were brutally murdered in their own bed. Eventually, Vonda's sixteen-year-old son was convicted of the slaying. Vonda's son, Sean Sellers, was also convicted of a previous murder of a convenience store clerk. When he was imprisoned, Sean was the youngest person ever to be on death row in Oklahoma.

A few years later while living in McAlester, Oklahoma, I was watching a live prime-time Geraldo Rivera special on NBC titled "Devil Worship: Exposing Satan's Underground." One of the guests appeared via satellite. While I sat in my living room, Sean Sellers sat across town on death row at the Oklahoma State Penitentiary. It had an eerie feeling when I realized I was watching a convicted killer who was only a couple of miles from me. On the show, Sean told his story of how he killed his parents as a human sacrifice to Satan. He was completing his task to break the tenth of the Ten Commandments. But Sean also proclaimed his conversion to Christianity. Much to Geraldo's chagrin, Sean started witnessing in an attempt to convert the nation.

Sean's passion for the faith led him eventually to write books in an attempt to help misguided teens. Still, in prison, he also started a web site for the same purpose. Prison officials have stated that he has been a model prisoner and has led Bible studies behind the walls.

At age 28, Sean made the news again. By this time I had relocated again. My local newspaper covered the story because Sean's uncle lived thirty miles from me. The paper reported on Sean's pleading a case of clemency before the parole board. He very humbly said at the hearing, "I can't imagine what I could say today to cause you to have mercy on me. The only thing I know to do is try to show my heart." He apologized at the hearing to his stepbrother. His uncle reportedly replied, "Stop begging. Take the punishment." Sean lost his case and was executed three days later.

I have always been a quiet advocate for capital punishment. I argued for it in a paper in an ethics class in seminary. And I've always been skeptical of prison-cell conversions. But somehow, for this case, it didn't seem right. I think I'm a fairly good judge of faith. To me, Sean Sellers seemed to be a man transformed by the grace of God.

Now don't get me wrong. What Sean Sellers did to his parents and a convenience store clerk were horrible acts. Murder is a terrible sin. But as Christians, how should we respond to this situation? As the bracelets constantly remind us to ask, "What would Jesus do?"

Murder is wrong. But so is hate — especially all-consuming hate that longs to see another die in the name of punishment. Especially unforgiving hate that doesn't consider transformation and grace.

What would Jesus do? I can't say for sure since I'm not Jesus. But I hear the words of Jesus ringing in my head. He saved the woman caught in adultery from certain execution and commanded her to live a changed life. He said, "Blessed are the merciful," in Matthew 5:7. I am sure that his actions would mirror the call of Micah 6:8 and involve fairness, love, kindness, and humility. It is what God requires of us as a response to our failures — the offering of our life lived in a Christ-like way.

Epiphany 5 / Ordinary Time 5
Matthew 5:13-20

An Act Of Obedience

"You are the light of the world. A city built on a hill cannot be hid. No one after lighting a lamp puts it under the bushel basket, but on the lampstand, and it gives light to all in the house. In the same way, let your light shine before others, so that they may see your good works and give glory to your Father in heaven." (vv. 14-16)

In 1998 the 200 employees of Inland Buildings in Cullman, Alabama, received startling news. The plant that produced custom engineered structural steel framing would have to lay off several employees. Kendall Smith began thinking about all the families who would be affected financially. He felt a call to pray for them. He invited a few other Inland employees to gather with him to pray about the situation. They would take ten minutes of their thirty-minute lunch break. They prayed for specific needs of employees and their families, the company, their churches, and the nation. They were elated when the layoffs ended in only two weeks.

However, the group continued to meet for prayer over the lunch break every Wednesday. Someone shares a brief devotion or scripture, and then they pray. Around 25 to 30 employees participate in the group.

Since the group began, they have prayed employees through many a trial. Jimmy Hyatt's four-year-old son, Jacob, went to Children's Hospital in Birmingham expecting treatment for a sinus problem. He was re-diagnosed with ependymoma and had a golf ball sized tumor removed from his brain. The prayer group not only prayed for the Hyatts, but they also took up a collection to help with their medical bills.

A similar event occurred with Dwight Oaks when his seven-year-old son, Josh, needed a kidney transplant. He didn't even have enough money to pay the deductible for the medication. He hoped for some kind of financial blessing. That night, his son found an envelope of money the prayer group had slipped into his lunch box.

Randall Cooksey's wife, Esther, developed a tumor that caused her excruciating abdominal pain. Doctors wouldn't know if it was cancerous until it was removed. The group prayed for Esther. Surgeons later removed a twelve-pound seven-ounce tumor. It was benign.

Cooksey has become a proponent of workplace prayer groups and has encouraged others to form groups in their places of employment. He sees a threefold benefit in the Inland group. First, the workplace has Christian witness. Second, the lives of the participants and their co-workers are blessed. And third, the nation is strengthened as they pray for our national leaders.

How easy it is to keep faith out of the workplace. Save it for Sunday. The group at Inland has chosen to be a light to the world, a lampstand, and a city on a hill. Their pre-Christian co-workers can't help but notice how they live out their faith as they show their good works for God's glory.

(Details taken from an October 2002 AFA Journal article by Randall Murphree.)

Epiphany 6 / Ordinary Time 6
Deuteronomy 30:15-20

Choose Life

I call heaven and earth to witness against you today that I have set before you life and death, blessings and curses. Choose life so that you and your descendants may live, loving the LORD your God, obeying him, and holding fast to him; for that means life to you and length of days, so that you may live in the land that the LORD swore to give to your ancestors, to Abraham, to Isaac, and to Jacob. (vv. 19-20)

Michael was the kind of guy who had such a positive outlook that you either loved him or hated him. When someone would ask him how he was doing, he would reply, "If I were any better, I would be twins!" He was a natural motivator. If a co-worker was having a bad day, Michael would encourage them and help them to see the positive side of the situation.

A friend asked how he could be so positive all the time. After all, it seemed so unnatural compared to the rest of the world. Michael replied, "Each morning I wake up and say to myself, 'You have two choices today. You can choose to be in a good mood or ... you can choose to be in a bad mood.' I choose to be in a good mood. Each time something bad happens, I can choose to be a victim or ... I can choose to learn from it. I choose to learn from it. Every time someone comes to me complaining, I can choose to accept their complaining or ... I can point out the positive side of life. I choose the positive side of life."

The friend protested that even though it sounded great in theory it would be hard to live out.

Michael responded, "Life is all about choices. When you cut away all the junk, every situation is a choice. You choose how you react to situations. You choose how people affect your mood. You choose to be in a good mood or bad mood. The bottom line: It's your choice how you live your life."

Several years later, Michael was involved in a serious accident as he fell sixty feet from a communications tower. As he lay on the ground, the first thing he thought of was the well-being of his soon-to-be-born daughter. Then, he remembered that he had two choices: He could choose to live or ... he could choose to die. He chose to live.

The paramedics arrived and went to work. They kept telling Michael that he was going to be fine. But when they wheeled him into the ER, he saw the expressions on the faces of the doctors and nurses. He began to feel fear overcoming his body because he could read their eyes: "He's a dead man." He knew he needed to take action.

A big burly nurse was shouting questions. She asked Michael if he was allergic to anything. He replied, "Yes." The doctors and nurses stopped working as they waited for Michael to fill in the missing blank of his allergy. He took a deep breath and yelled, "Gravity." Over their laughter, he said, "I am choosing to live. Operate on me with that understanding."

After eighteen hours of surgery and weeks of intensive care, Michael was released from the hospital with rods placed in his back. Michael lived, thanks to the skill of his doctors, and also because of his amazing attitude. When asked about his health, Michael would respond, "If I were any better, I'd be twins. Want to see my scars?"

Epiphany 7 / Ordinary Time 7
Matthew 5:38-48

An Enemy Loved

> *"You have heard that it was said, 'You shall love your neighbor and hate your enemy.' But I say to you, Love your enemies and pray for those who persecute you, so that you may be children of your Father in heaven; for he makes his sun rise on the evil and on the good, and sends rain on the righteous and on the unrighteous. For if you love those who love you, what reward do you have? Do not even the tax collectors do the same? And if you greet only your brothers and sisters, what more are you doing than others? Do not even the Gentiles do the same?" (vv. 43-47)*

As a minister, I am called to love my neighbor and to love my enemies. As a member of the human race, I find it's not always easy. A case in point is a woman in a previous congregation. I'll call her Sally to shield her identity although it's hardly necessary. Sally has done so many unique mean-spirited things it would be nearly impossible not to recognize her if you know her. It's hard to forget a seventy-something squatty little bulldog of a woman with an eternal scowl on her face. Her photo in our church directory looks like she could jump out of the picture any minute and rip your heart out. She is so angry and bitter that I'm not sure her tough exterior doesn't go to the core. I've often said you could designate a day in her honor, and Sally would find some reason to complain about it.

I know these words sound harsh, but let her actions paint a picture of her for you. Not long after I met her, we were in a church meeting. I mentioned that we needed a teacher for an ongoing Bible study. A retired minister promptly volunteered. Sally, who was sitting behind him, responded loudly and belligerently. **"No. No. No. No. No."** Her response sounded like a freight train if your ear was directly on the whistle. One "no" would have been sufficient to express her opinion. I guess the others were for emphasis. I'm not sure about the cause of the protest since she didn't even attend the Bible study.

Twice during the celebration of our church's "joys" in our worship service, she went in attack mode and griped me out for something she felt I mishandled. Some joy. It embarrassed most of the church members, and I hate to think what the episode impressed upon our visitors. However, it also garnered the usual response, "That's just Sally." It was our feeble attempt to act like we are addressing the problem when we were not.

But the zenith of her dysfunction occurred following a church meeting. Once again Sally verbally attacked another church member in a meeting. The victim this time was a frail, elderly woman pushing ninety. This offended the victim's son who was also in the meeting. The son, a large man in his late fifties, foolishly followed Sally to her car and insisted on an explanation as to why she hated his mother. As she got into her car, she responded, "I don't hate your mother."

But as my mama used to say, "Actions speak louder than words." It was obvious Sally hated his mother. It was obvious Sally hated everything and everybody. The son still insisted on an answer and positioned himself between Sally and the still open car door. Sally was now stuck. She couldn't close her door, and therefore, couldn't close the conversation. I don't know what Sally was thinking, or if she was thinking. But she reached up and punched the 250-pound man in the nose. The man was stunned. Sally closed her door and drove off.

It's hard to love Sally. But God said to love your enemies, so I prayed for Sally — often, very often. I do my Christian duty, you know. One Sunday though, my wife, Hadley, reminded me what loving an enemy really means. Hadley was sitting in worship and was compelled to say three important words to Sally. She went to Sally during our "meeting and greeting" time, and said, "I love you." Sally couldn't have been more stunned had it been a punch in the nose. She murmured something like, "Oh, yeah, well uh." Then Hadley interrupted her stammering, "I just thought you should know that you are loved." Quietly, Hadley walked away.

It was a reminder to me that when God asks us to love our neighbors, actions speak louder than prayers. Sure, we are supposed to pray. But we're also supposed to act. We should not only tell people we love them, but also show them. Who's your enemy? Have you told them you love them — and meant it?

I don't know how much of it had to do with Hadley's words, but Sally has become a changed person. She offers input instead of insults in meetings now. What a testimony of God's redeeming grace that transforms us into new creations.

Epiphany 8 / Ordinary Time 8
Matthew 6:24-34

The Lord Provides

"Therefore do not worry, saying, 'What will we eat?' or 'What will we drink?' or 'What will we wear?' For it is the Gentiles who strive for all these things; and indeed your heavenly Father knows that you need all these things. But strive first for the kingdom of God and his righteousness, and all these things will be given to you as well. So do not worry about tomorrow, for tomorrow will bring worries of its own. Today's trouble is enough for today." (vv. 31-34)

When I was in junior high and high school, my family watched *Little House on the Prairie*. I wouldn't admit it to my friends in high school, but I enjoyed the show. There was something wholesome and spiritual about it. Although the Ingles family endured a lot of tragedy, somehow they would always land on their feet. It was a terrible year for crops; the patriarch Charles Ingles would say, "The Lord will provide." Then a job opened up in the sawmill. No matter what the tragedy, Charles had only one response: "The Lord will provide." And sure enough, God provided a way. It seemed like this was the plot about every third episode.

One of my favorite episodes saw the tables turned on Charles. His oldest daughter Mary, who had become blind, was now married and ran a school for blind children with her husband. The school was in need of a new facility and had very little money for rent. Charles was on a trip to the city with his other daughter, Laura, whom he called "Half-pint." As they were driving their two-horse wagon, they looked down to the end of the street and saw an old abandoned building with a "For Sale" sign hanging in the window. Laura remarked to her father how perfect the building would be for the blind school. He questioned where the money would come from. Without hesitation, she responded, "As you always say, Pa, the Lord will provide."

If I'm truthful, I liked that episode because a teenager, like myself at the time, had proved a point to an adult. Now as an adult and a father, I like it because it suggests that children eventually learn our belief system. What more valuable lesson is there than to hold so dear a faith in God? Well, none.

Unlike *Little House on the Prairie*, the providence of God and God's love for humanity are more than just fiction. Yesterday I was at my Rotary Club meeting and Richard Williams, who is the director of The Mission Society for United Methodists, brought our program. His group sends dental and medical missionaries to third world countries. Williams told how they had healed thousands of people — first physically and then spiritually — in Africa and South America. But he also told a story of how God provided for their ministry.

When this ministry was first beginning, it became apparent to Dr. Jeff Lester, the Mission Society's founder, that they needed a portable CAT scanner. Dr. Lester called the CEO of a company that manufactures CAT scanners and asked if he could donate a machine to their mission ministry. The CEO replied, "No. If I gave one to your organization then I would have to give one to every other organization that requests one. We simply cannot afford to give away that many CAT scanners no matter how benevolent the organization."

A few weeks later, a call came that the CAT scanner was being sent with instructions on where to pick it up. Mission Society volunteers retrieved the machine from the pick up point. After the machine arrived, Dr. Lester called the CEO to thank him for his change of heart. The CEO didn't know what Dr. Lester was talking about. His company had not sent the CAT scanner. To this day, the origin of the CAT scanner remains a mystery.

Praise God they received their CAT scanner because it has helped heal a lot of people. The Lord provided. And praise God I was at my Rotary meeting, because just as I had decided to write this book and wondered if I had enough God stories to write about, the Lord provided me with this story to share with you. The Lord does provide. To those of faith, that is no mystery. We have a blessed assurance of that.

The Transfiguration Of Our Lord / Last Sunday After Epiphany
Matthew 17:1-9

How Big Is He?

While he was still speaking, suddenly a bright cloud overshadowed them, and from the cloud a voice said, "This is my Son, the Beloved; with him I am well pleased; listen to him!" When the disciples heard this, they fell to the ground and were overcome by fear. But Jesus came and touched them, saying, "Get up and do not be afraid." And when they looked up, they saw no one except Jesus himself alone. (vv. 5-8)

The Pope allegedly was flying from Rome to New York for a very important meeting with the Secretary General of the United Nations. Preparations for the meeting had begun months earlier, and the Pope eagerly anticipated his part in this historic meeting.

As the plane approached John F. Kennedy Airport in New York City, it was unexpectedly diverted to Newark Airport in New Jersey. Then because of unsafe wind conditions, the aircraft was forced into a holding pattern, which further delayed the arrival for more than an hour. When the plane finally touched down at Newark, the Pope was quickly whisked away in a limousine to his conference with the Secretary General at the U.N. building in Midtown Manhattan.

With the meeting scheduled to begin within a few minutes, the Pope sat anxiously in the back seat of the limousine. He then gently asked the chauffeur, "Can you drive a bit faster, my son? I have a meeting with the Secretary General of the United Nations. There are more than 200 dignitaries awaiting my arrival. The outcome of this meeting could have a dramatic effect on world events. I must not be late."

The limousine driver begged, "I'm terribly sorry, Your Holiness, but I can't afford another speeding ticket. I have already been warned that if I receive one more ticket I will lose my license. Surely you understand. I have a wife and three children to support. I'm really terribly sorry."

The Pope was sympathetic to the worried driver. However, he desperately needed to travel faster. He asked the chauffeur to stop the car. The Pope then got out of the limousine, told the chauffeur to get in the back, and then stepped in behind the wheel himself as he sped off toward his appointment.

The Pope drove aggressively and rapidly wove in and out of traffic. His driving caught the attention of several motorists, none more important than two New York City police officers. The officers promptly chased the vehicle and signaled it to pull over.

A notoriously tough officer announced to his partner, "Let me handle this one. These big shots think they can order their chauffeurs to speed around my city in their big limousines. Well, this one's not going to get away with it. I'll see to that. Before I'm through, this guy will have at least five tickets to pay! It'll be the sorriest day of his life."

His partner remained in the patrol car and watched. Within a minute, the hard-nosed cop returned and was visibly shaken. His ticket book was still unopened. His partnered inquired, "You didn't write him a single ticket? What happened?"

The first officer said sheepishly, "I couldn't write him a ticket. This guy is important. I mean really important."

His partner asked, "Who was it? The Mayor of New York City?"

The first officer responded, "No, bigger than that."

His partner then asked, "Well, was it the Governor of New York State?"

He replied, "No, bigger than that."

His partner cried out, "Don't tell me you pulled over the President of the United States?"

The shaken cop insisted, "No, he's even bigger than that!"

His partner retorted, "Bigger than the President of the United States? Who in the world is bigger than the President of The United States?"

The first officer answered, "Well, I'm not exactly sure, but the Pope is his chauffeur!"

Peter, James, and John might have wondered who was bigger than Moses and Elijah. God let them know it was Jesus, God's Beloved Son. The importance of Elijah and Moses faded away when placed next to Jesus.

Ash Wednesday
Matthew 6:1-6, 16-21

The Rescuers

"Beware of practicing your piety before others in order to be seen by them; for then you have no reward from your Father in heaven." (v. 1)

I was driving one Thursday morning from Heavener, Oklahoma, to a meeting in McAlester, Oklahoma. As I often do when I drive long distances, I was multitasking. In this case, the drive was an hour and a half, and my second task was to organize upcoming ministries. My thoughts were on the church's ministry committee's dinner the next Sunday evening and the upcoming newsletter articles. In particular, I was trying to figure out what I would write for my column. Then it came to me by accident — literally.

I guess with the intermittent rain and sleet, I hit a slick spot on this paved county road I take as a shortcut. I crossed the eastbound lane and was heading into the ditch when I swerved back on the road. I crossed both lanes and went into the other ditch. I was better off with the first ditch because it was really an open field. However, my chosen path (for lack of a better term) was a thicket of saplings — several small trees an inch or so in diameter — and a barbed wire fence. For ten to fifteen yards, I plowed over the brush and scraped the fence. When I finally stopped, I was trapped. In front of me was five yards of sapling trees. These little trees were also pressed up against both driver side doors. The barbed wire fence prevented the passenger side doors from opening. Since the driver's window sometimes acts up, I had to crawl to the back and exit through one of the back windows.

The first vehicle that approached stopped to help. So did the second. As did the third who actually had the ability to help — a truck and chains. The second guy left when he thought everything was under control. But then we discovered the chain wasn't long enough to reach from the road to my car. So my first rescuer went to get another chain. That left me with the three people in the truck who had stopped to pull me out — a married couple and a second woman. As we talked, it was apparent that the three probably weren't Christian. They used PG-13 language and indicated that their Wednesday night social wasn't a fellowship dinner. It's amazing how people don't censor themselves when they think you're a student at the local junior college.

After learning I wasn't a student, one woman asked what I did for a living. I told them I was a minister. One of the women asked, "What's that? That's not a preacher or something, is it?" The other woman assured her that a minister was indeed a preacher. I told them that I hoped I didn't make them feel uncomfortable. They assured me I didn't, but I could tell it was a little white lie. Funny, how the conversation held a "G" rating after my occupation was revealed. Finally, the second chain arrived. But before leaving I agreed to pay the couple back by helping them renew their vows on their anniversary, which was a few months away. I gave them my card, and we'll see if they call.

I was struck by the encounter. All the people who stopped to help me were hard-living folks. It was 9:45 a.m. and they weren't at work, which meant they didn't have nine-to-five jobs. Some people who live off this county road are farmers and ranchers. Others live out there simply because it keeps a distance between them and the law. Who were these rescuers that came to my aid? I don't know. As I've said, based on their demeanor, I doubted that they were Christian. However, what was apparent was that their actions were very Christ-like. In fact, every vehicle that passed that way slowed down to make sure everybody was okay. They weren't looking for glory. They were all just helping to help. It made me pray that all Christians, including myself, would be as Christ-like in helping others.

Lent 1
Genesis 2:15-17; 3:1-7

Making Mistakes

So when the woman saw that the tree was good for food, and that it was a delight to the eyes, and that the tree was to be desired to make one wise, she took of its fruit and ate; and she also gave some to her husband, who was with her, and he ate. Then the eyes of both were opened, and they knew that they were naked; and they sewed fig leaves together and made loincloths for themselves. (vv. 6-7)

There once was a young princess who never laughed. She wouldn't even smile. As her parents, the king and queen brought jesters and other entertainers to the castle to try to make her laugh, promising gold if they did. None of their funny faces or silly costumes ever made her laugh. She didn't even crack a smile.

Now, near the castle lived a poor woman and her son. They were near starvation, so the poor woman said to her son, "Go to the castle and see if they will give you a job."

The boy very diligently went to the castle to find work. He was strong, but not very bright. The first day he went to work at the royal chicken coop. All day he gathered eggs. At the end of the day, the royal chicken keeper gave him some fresh eggs to take home. The boy carried them in his hands as he walked home, but he didn't watch where he was going. He tripped on a rock, and the eggs flew into the air. He tried to catch the eggs as he was falling, but he missed them all. Some even landed on his head. The princess witnessed the entire episode, but she didn't laugh.

When he got home with egg all over his face, his mother asked, "Why didn't you carry the eggs in your hat? They would have been safe, and you probably wouldn't have tripped because you could watch where you were going."

The next day, the boy went back to the castle to work. They sent him to the royal dairy. He milked cows all day, and when he was finished the royal cow keeper gave him a pail of fresh milk to take home. Remembering that his mother told him to carry the eggs in his hat, he poured the milk into his hat to carry it home! The princess saw him with his leaky hat of milk. She still didn't laugh.

His mother yelled at him when he got home, "Why did you pour it in your hat? You should have carried the pail in your hands!"

The next day the boy went back to the castle. This time they sent him to the swineherd to help feed the royal pigs. He fed the pigs all day, and then at the end of the day, he was given a squirmy little pig to take home.

The princess looked out of her window, and saw the silly boy trying to carry the pig in his hands, muttering, "My mother told me to carry it in my hands." She watched as the pig squirmed out of his hands and ran away. The silly boy chased the pig, but the princess still didn't laugh.

When he got home, his mother chastised him, and told him, "You should have pulled the pig home with a rope tied around its neck!"

The next day the boy worked in the castle kitchen washing dishes. When he was done, the royal cook gave him a great big fish to take home to his mother. Remembering his mother's advice, he tied a rope around the fish and dragged it home. Cats followed behind him and ate the fish as he walked. The princess saw all this from her window, but she still didn't smile.

Once again at home, his mother advised him. She said, "We have nothing to eat! If only you had carried the fish on your shoulder."

So the next day the boy went to the castle and went to work cleaning the royal barn. He worked so hard that the royal cow keeper gave him a cow to take home. The boy was so excited because they would have milk every day. He remembered what his mother said about carrying the fish on his shoulder, so he got down on his hands and knees and crawled under the cow. He tried to stand up with the cow on his shoulder.

The princess witnessed this strange sight, and she burst out laughing. She laughed so loudly that the king and the queen ran to her room. Upon discovering that the boy made her laugh, the king and queen invited the boy and his mother to live in the castle and keep the princess laughing. They were never poor again.

So many times we try to do the right thing but end up making a mistake. Because God is a God of grace, often things will eventually work out all right. However, the mistakes can prove so costly in the meantime.

Lent 2
John 3:1-17

A New Spiritual Birth

> *Jesus answered, "Very truly, I tell you, no one can enter the kingdom of God without being born of water and Spirit. What is born of the flesh is flesh, and what is born of the Spirit is spirit ... For God so loved the world that he gave his only Son, so that everyone who believes in him may not perish but may have eternal life." (vv. 5-6, 16)*

John was the son of a minister, and learned the faith at his mother's knee. He studied to be a minister at a very prestigious university. While in college, he organized a Bible study group that also helped feed the poor and visited the imprisoned.

After he was ordained, he moved to Savannah, Georgia, where he became the minister of a local church for his denomination. A young woman in his congregation, Sophia Hopkey, began to study the Bible with John. They were romantically attracted to each other, but John was hesitant to proceed. She was a member of his congregation, which posed one problem. Another was that John was not sure about marriage. He wondered if he could be an effective minister if he had responsibilities to a wife and possibly children. John was torn between two lovers — Sophia and the ministry. The nature of his relationship with Sophia was never clearly defined.

Sophia became tired of John's indecision and apparent disinterest. She began seeing another man. That relationship led to a proposal of marriage. After stalling in hopes that John would finally admit his love for her, she accepted the proposal and was married.

Sophia and her new husband attended John's church. John knew he had made a mistake with Sophia. Instead of confessing it, he took his frustration out on the newlyweds. With a flimsy excuse, he refused to serve the couple communion one Sunday. The couple became irate and began the process to have John removed as the pastor of the church. But before any decisions were formally made, John desperately left Savannah in the middle of the night.

John questioned his faith, his calling, and his own salvation. On his return trip home, he met a group of Christians who shared with him their belief of grace — that God loved the world enough that a simple passionate belief in Jesus would save humanity.

When John arrived home, he went to a Bible study with some of the Christians he met on his return trip. That night they studied the book of Romans. John experienced a new birth. He described it saying, "I felt my heart strangely warmed. I felt I did trust in Christ, Christ alone for salvation: And an assurance was given me, that he had taken away *my* sins, even *mine*, and saved *me* from the law of sin and death."

This John — the jilted lover and minister who was born anew — was John Wesley, the founder of Methodism.

Lent 3
John 4:5-42

Rag Pickers Of Juarez

Jesus answered her, "If you knew the gift of God, and who it is saying to you, 'Give me a drink,' you would have asked him, and he would have given you living water." (v. 10)

In a December 1995 *Guidepost* devotional, John Sherrill tells of the struggle to survive by some of the most impoverished people in Mexico. In the dumps outside of Juarez, Mexico, some of the destitute would scavenge through the garbage looking for anything of value. The value didn't have to be great; it only needed to be enough to bring in a little income. The Mexicans who scavenged the dumps were known as the "rag pickers of Juarez." Most rag pickers live in cardboard houses with no running water. In the sweltering heat of summer, it is not unusual for people to die of dehydration.

Across the border in the desert just outside El Paso, Texas, is a ministry called The Lord's Ranch. In an attempt to keep the rag pickers from dehydrating, they provide water to them. The ranch sits on an aquifer that supplies abundant water. At the ranch, the rag pickers could take two showers a week.

Mary Ann Halloran works with the rag pickers at The Lord's Ranch. One day several years ago, a young man with cracked, parched lips came to the back door. He asked for a glass of water, and Mary Ann obliged. The man drank the water, and with an intense look, he told her, "Never, never forget that water is a gift." Then he walked away.

Many Ann was stunned by the man's words. She stood immobilized by their significance. As she awakened from the trance, she realized that she should have offered the man something to eat.

She ran outside to find him. She looked ahead and to her left and to her right. The desert was vast but open. The man was nowhere in sight. She went to her car, got in, and drove down the road looking for the stranger. He was still nowhere to be found. He had vanished.

Mary Ann pulled the car to the side of the road. She thought, "The man with the parched lips had come to bring a message. Not just to The Lord's Ranch, but to everyone. Water is precious ... it is a gift of God."

Lent 4
John 9:1-41

Daniel

> *When he had said this, he spat on the ground and made mud with the saliva and spread the mud on the man's eyes, saying to him. "Go, wash in the pool of Siloam" (which means Sent). Then he went and washed and came back able to see. (vv. 6-7)*

It was a beautiful Saturday night in June, and seventeen-year-old Daniel jumped into his pickup after saying good night to his girlfriend. He had just enough time to make it home before his midnight curfew. It had been an exciting day spent cooling off from the summer sun by swimming. He was driving south on state highway 54, barefoot and still wearing his swimsuit without a T-shirt.

It was dark on the desolate little highway — so dark that Daniel didn't see the black cow that had wondered onto the pavement. He slammed on the brakes, but it was too late. He hit the cow and the pickup started to flip. Since he wasn't wearing his seat belt, he was thrown through the windshield. His head hit the pavement, and then, his scantily clad body skidded across the caustic surface. The momentum of the ejection finally slowed, and Daniel came to a stop. He was barely conscious, but he was aware enough to move himself commando style to the side of the road. He wanted to avoid traffic although there was hardly any on the highway so late at night.

In fact, Daniel lay by the side of the highway for forty minutes until someone drove by, saw his truck, and then found him. As they were loading him in the ambulance, his parents drove upon the scene as they were now retracing Daniel's steps. He was rushed to the hospital thirty miles away.

Daniel's church was buzzing the next day with the news of the accident. The minister went to the hospital after the service. The first person he saw was Daniel's grandmother. Her face revealed that she was reliving the experience of another grandson who was paralyzed because of a car wreck about a year earlier.

Daniel was in ICU with severe head trauma. He was alive, but unconscious. The extent of the damage was unknown, but the doctors were hopeful. Over the next few weeks, Daniel began to regain consciousness, but only for brief periods of time. With slurred speech, he would identify the people in the room. He recognized the minister but couldn't recall his name. He simply called him Preacher. It became apparent that recovery would be a long process. His mind was like that of a child, and he would have to start over with his education. He would probably miss his senior year of high school just to relearn the basics in life such as walking, talking, eating, and dressing. After a month-long stay in the local hospital, Daniel would be transferred to a specialized rehabilitation center in Dallas. As soon as the paperwork was cleared, Daniel was moved.

At the end of the week, the minister was shopping at Wal-Mart with his family. While pushing the cart past the men's wear section, he was surprised when Daniel's dad stepped into the aisle. The father was equally surprised to see the minister and his family. He simply asked the minister and family to follow him. He led them to the pharmacy where Daniel was picking up a prescription with his mother and his brother. Daniel had been released from the rehabilitation center. What was supposed to be months of rehabilitation turned out to be a week. The doctors couldn't explain it. The area on his brain that was bruised had mysteriously cleared up on its own. Daniel's motor skills were still a little slow, but they were functioning normally.

Two days later, the minister fully expected to see Daniel and his family in worship. He was a little disappointed to walk into the sanctuary as the service started and see their regular pew still empty. But dismay soon turned to a joy. As soon as the congregation began to sing the chorus of the first hymn, the family walked in. The timing couldn't have been more perfect. Shivers went up and down many a spine as they sang "O victory in Jesus, my savior forever!"

The doctors couldn't medically explain Daniel's recovery. But it was obvious to the church people. After all, they sang about it in the hymn. There is victory in Jesus. In this case, that victory meant the physical healing of a young man. Thanks be to God.

Lent 5
Romans 8:6-11

God Is Our Security Guard

To set the mind on the flesh is death, but to set the mind on the Spirit is life and peace. (v. 6)

Dorothy Nicholas and her husband tell their story in *His Mysterious Ways, Vol. II*. The couple was originally from Greenwood, South Carolina, but after they retired, they moved south to sunny Florida. One day, they were visiting with their next-door neighbors around their kitchen table. Their young neighbors had helped them a lot over the previous year and a half. Dorothy had suffered a stroke and her husband had injured his leg. Without these good neighbors, the Nicolas' healing would have been more difficult.

During the conversation this day, the young husband unexpectedly began telling them the story of his troubled past. He, too, was originally from Greenwood, South Carolina. At age sixteen he was hanging out with a rough crowd and getting into trouble with the law. His activities led him to a year in a juvenile reformatory. When he was released, he had good intentions of turning his life around. He struggled, though, because of his record, which scared away potential employers. With feelings of desperation and hopelessness, he decided to hold up a local service station. He thought he could get enough money to leave the state and start over. So he stole a car and a gun from his father. He drove up to the service station just before closing time. The manager was a woman, which comforted him because he thought she would cooperate.

Before he initiated the robbery, he looked up and saw a sign attached to the roof of the service station. It read, "God Is Our Security Guard — Always On The Job." It stopped him in his tracks. It was a sign telling him not to go through with the robbery. He then hurried home and prayed the rest of the night. The whole experience gave him the focus to turn his life around. Through prayer and faith, he was able to.

Dorothy and her husband were in shock. They simply looked at each other for tenuous moments. Both knew what the other was thinking. Thirteen years before, Dorothy sat at their kitchen table in Greenwood, South Carolina, trying to come up with a catchy sign for their business. She had scribbled down several phrases but nothing seemed right. Then finally she wrote down the words that her husband put on a sign over their service station: God Is Our Security Guard — Always On The Job.

Had the young neighbor set his mind on the flesh and robbed the service station, he would have continued on a road of death. But the glorious sign set his mind on the Spirit, which led to his life of peace.

Sunday Of The Passion / Palm Sunday
Matthew 27:11-54

The Maiden Who Seeks Her Brothers

Now Jesus stood before the governor; and the governor asked him, "Are you the King of the Jews?" Jesus said, "You say so." But when he was accused by the chief priests and elders, he did not answer. Then Pilate said to him, "Do you not hear how many accusations they make against you?" But he gave him no answer, not even to a single charge, so that the governor was greatly amazed. (vv. 11-14)

The Grimm Brothers told the folktale of a king and a queen who had twelve sons. The king desperately wanted a daughter. His obsession was maddening. When the queen became pregnant, the king told her, "If this child is a girl, I will kill all our boys and let her inherit our kingdom and all our riches all by herself."

The queen was terrified at her husband's plans, but she was also terribly afraid of her husband. Eventually, the queen gave birth to a daughter. Fortunately, their youngest son, Benjamin, had learned about his father's dastardly plan, and the twelve brothers escaped the castle before the king could execute them. They hid deep in the forest where they scarcely saw other people. The twelve brothers were so angry that they vowed to kill the first girl they met.

Ten years passed, and the baby grew into a little girl. One day, the girl discovered twelve shirts in the castle. She asked about them and learned of her twelve brothers. She was shocked at the insanity of the truth, and she renounced her inheritance. She set out to search for her brothers, taking the shirts with her.

A few days later, she found the cottage where they lived. Benjamin was home alone as the rest of the brothers were out hunting. She told him the story and showed him the shirts. He knew undoubtedly this was his sister. Remembering the horrible promise his brothers had made to kill the first girl they saw, Benjamin hid his sister under a big tub.

When his older brothers returned to eat dinner, Benjamin told them he had great news. They asked him to share his news. Benjamin agreed to tell them only if the other brothers would agree to end the promise to kill the first girl they met. Once they agreed, he shouted, "Our sister is here!" as he lifted the tub covering her. They all embraced her and begged her to stay with them. Having renounced her inheritance, she agreed.

One day the girl was picking flowers near the cottage. She unknowingly picked twelve cursed flowers. As she picked each one, each of her twelve brothers was turned into a raven and flew away. The girl sought out a wise woman who told the girl that the only way to break the magic spell was for her to remain silent for seven years. If she spoke during that time, her brothers would die. The girl vowed to keep silent all those years.

Nearly seven years passed, when a young king rode through the woods, met the girl, and fell in love with her. He asked her to be his queen and marry him. She replied by nodding her head yes, but said not a word.

The king's mother did not like her son's wife. She was a forest girl who didn't talk. The mother falsely accused the girl of having done all sorts of evil things. The seven years were almost passed, but not quite. The girl would not say a word in her defense. The mother's word was believed, and the girl was condemned to death.

She was taken to the courtyard and tied to a stake. Wood was piled around her and set on fire, and yet she still did not say a word. The flames began to creep toward her. Suddenly, twelve ravens came flying into the courtyard. As each touched the ground, it turned into one of her brothers. They all raced to her, kicking away the wood and untying her.

Now their sister could explain that she had a reason for not speaking — to save her brothers. She had done none of the things of which she was accused. Her husband, the king, rejoiced, and they all lived happily ever after.

Maundy Thursday / Holy Thursday
John 13:1-17, 31b-35

Al Webster: The Gentle Giant

Jesus, knowing that the Father had given all things into his hands, and that he had come from God and was going to God, got up from the table, took off his outer robe, and tied a towel around himself. Then he poured water into a basin and began to wash the disciples' feet and to wipe them with the towel that was tied around him. (vv. 3-5)

For four years I went to college with a gentle giant named Al Webster. By external standards, he was not a handsome guy; he had a blond Afro and thick, Coke-bottle glasses. But Al's soul is the most beautiful that I have ever known. I call Al a giant because he stood about six-feet-one-inch tall, and his shoulders were as broad as a doorway. Al would often give his friends an affectionate high-five that would send pain tingling down the arm. The stinging could last a week. Whenever we would comment on how big Al was, he would quietly remind us that he was the runt of his family. I was the runt of mine too, but I wasn't close to Al's size. Being a runt is relative.

Over the years I kept in touch with Al. I moved away to Fort Worth to attend seminary. Big Al helped my wife and me make the four-hour move. Later, Al would just drop in. It seemed one of his larger brothers lived in a Fort Worth suburb. We never knew when Al would call and say, "I'll be over in ten minutes."

In college Al majored in religion, but his hobby was working with computers. After college, he turned his hobby into a career working as a part-time computer/Internet consultant. He pretty much lived hand-to-mouth. His real dream was to preserve the Cherokee language by developing a Cherokee talking dictionary. The plan was to record each Cherokee word on computer so that younger Cherokees could hear it with the touch of a button. I have to admit when he first told me of his plan, I didn't think it made much sense. First of all, he wasn't Cherokee or even Native American for that matter. Secondly, I couldn't see that it was profitable.

However, Al was successful with his Cherokee talking dictionary. He even started working with other tribes — Creek, Choctaw, and Osage. He developed a computer software package with all 85 characters of the Cherokee language. The software enabled the Cherokee to publish in their own language. His system became the standard for writing Cherokee. Another computer program he developed on Native American languages is in the Smithsonian Institute. Never stand in the way of a dreamer.

But that didn't matter to Al. His concern for the project wasn't financial. Al was a servant, and people were more important than money. Al was known to literally give away the coat off his back and spend his last dollar on food for a vagabond. Once Al was visiting a Native American school for the purpose of selling his software. The teacher was impressed, but she wasn't interested in the software. The school couldn't afford a computer, let alone the software. So Al left empty handed. Literally. He gave them his Macintosh Power Book. When asked about it, he said, "They needed it more than I did." With Al's love of computers, he might as well have given away his brain or a kidney.

Because people came first with Al, he had a habit of being tardy — if someone needed help, he would stop no matter what. All his friends referred to his tardiness as "Al time." If you were meeting Al, you would tell him the appointment was an hour earlier so he would actually show up on time. But when he did arrive, he would pass on the story of the person he stopped to help. This was usually a new acquaintance — "new" meaning he had just met them when he helped them. Talk about your Good Samaritan.

A few years ago, I attended our annual conference meeting in Tulsa. Al attended the closing worship service with me. At the conclusion of the service around 9 p.m., I went to the parking lot and discovered that I had a flat tire on my truck. I stood distraught in the dark still wearing my suit, white shirt, and dress shoes. Al insisted on changing the flat tire because he was wearing more casual clothes. Later, it hit me that I had contributed to "Al time." I wondered what I made him late for that night.

As you might have noticed, I speak of Al in the past tense. I do because Al passed away August 15, 1997, at the age of 31. He was killed when his Nissan truck went under the trailer of an 18-wheeler. No one knows why for sure, but Al failed to stop at a highway intersection. Since he was headed west and it was 7:15 p.m., some suspect the sun blinded him. Al's death was tragic, but in a beautiful twist of fate, he died living his dream. The fatality occurred as Al was driving home after meeting with Leaford Bearskin, chief of the Wyandottes, to preserve his language on computer.

I write this not as a eulogy, but as a testimony. Al was definitely God's handiwork. So many people didn't have the opportunity to know this low-key Christ-like man. Al was written about in *The Smithsonian* because of his efforts with the Cherokee talking dictionary, but that would only tell such a small part of the story of this gentle giant. *The Smithsonian* wouldn't tell of Al's compassion and faith.

A homeless Cherokee man once stopped in Al's church and interrupted a men's meeting. The men helped the homeless man, and then he left. At some point, they noticed Al was no longer there. They thought he had gone home, but as they were leaving, they found him outside the church with the homeless man. Al was softly singing the Lord's Prayer in Cherokee with the man. Al was not content just to feed the man's stomach. He also wanted to feed his soul.

As I stood at the funeral home seeing the body of my good friend lying in a casket, I cried. I didn't cry because he died so young. With Al's strong faith, he was happy in heaven. I didn't cry because I lost a good friend. Our geographical distance allowed us to see each other only a couple times a year. I cried because the world lost a great servant.

In the days following his funeral, I pledged to tell Al's story. Al was a man of great faith who was generous with his time, talent, and material things. The way he lived his life is a lesson in love, selflessness, and compassion. These are subjects we often flunk in a me-first world. I struggled to learn all Al had to teach me about compassionate faith and servanthood. By the grace of God, I am still learning from the life of Al Webster. Hopefully, you are learning from him as well.

Good Friday
John 18:1—19:42

Simpson

Then Pilate took Jesus and had him flogged. And the soldiers wove a crown of thorns and put it on his head, and they dressed him in a purple robe. They kept coming up to him, saying, "Hail, King of the Jews!" and striking him on the face. Pilate went out again and said to them, "Look, I am bringing him out to you to let you know that I find no case against him." So Jesus came out, wearing the crown of thorns and the purple robe. Pilate said to them, "Here is the man!" When the chief priests and the police saw him, they shouted, "Crucify him! Crucify him!" (19:1-6a)

Steve and Maria Garner wrote a song named "Simpson" based on a true story. In the song, they reflect on being eleven years old and making fun of a boy named Leonard Simpson who lived in the neighborhood. There were a lot of reasons for picking on Simpson. He was obese. His father gave him haircuts. He wore bibbed overalls with sleeveless underwear and high-topped army boots. He also had a crush on the not-so-pretty girl who lived next door to him. Yeah, Simpson was an easy target — a fat kid who looked funny and had ugly friends. The neighborhood kids even developed a chant: "Fatty, fatty, fatty, fatty two-by-four. We saw you hug the ugly girl next door."

At one point, the neighborhood kids played a cruel prank on Simpson. They invited him to join their club. On the clubhouse door, they wrote his name like the other members, and just as he thought the popular kids in the neighborhood might accept him, they threw mud at Simpson's name. Not only did they cover Simpson's name, but they also covered any hope he had of belonging.

Well, life went on. The children grew up and went different directions. Eighteen years passed before the Garners heard about Leonard Simpson again. Simpson witnessed a young African-American boy being picked on by a gang. Undoubtedly because he had endured similar cruel treatment as a youngster, Simpson couldn't stand idly by. He jumped into the fracas to protect the young boy. In the process, the gang beat Simpson to death with chains. The obese kid, who dressed oddly, died as a hero.

In the last stanza of the song, the Garners reflect on life — how there are successes and losses. Mainly they reflect on the parallel between the death of Leonard Simpson and the death of Jesus Christ. Both had been misunderstood and treated cruelly. Both had been unmercifully mocked. Both had been flogged and died tragically at a young age. But what is most important, both gave their lives so that others might live.

The Resurrection Of Our Lord / Easter Sunday
Matthew 28:1-10

Breaking The Stone

After the sabbath, as the first day of the week was dawning, Mary Magdalene and the other Mary went to see the tomb. And suddenly there was a great earthquake; for an angel of the Lord, descending from heaven, came and rolled back the stone and sat on it. His appearance was like lightning, and his clothing white as snow. For fear of him the guards shook and became like dead men. But the angel said to the women, "Do not be afraid; I know that you are looking for Jesus who was crucified. He is not here; for he has been raised, as he said." (vv. 1-6)

Moishe Rosen founded Jews for Jesus, an organization that aims to evangelize Jews to a belief that Jesus is the Messiah. In a newsletter article titled "Resurrection Reflections," he reflects on his conversion to Christ. His wife, Ceil, had a budding faith in Jesus. As a Jew, he struggled with her new faith. He went to Rabbi Brycks who had married the couple for advice on how to dissuade Ceil's new beliefs. Rabbi Brycks was Orthodox, good-natured, and easy to talk to.

Rosen said, "I need to know the official Jewish reasons for not believing in Jesus." He was prepared to receive a deep theological answer.

Rabbi Brycks replied with a long "W-e-e-l-l-l." After a brief pause, he said, "It's just something that you can't believe." Rosen waited, hoping there was some more substantial reasoning. Rabbi Brycks continued, "Christians think that God made a virgin pregnant, and from that they got Jesus."

Rosen replied, "So." He figured that if God could create the universe out of nothing, arranging for a virgin to be pregnant wouldn't be problematic.

Rabbi Brycks resumed, "And Judaism is a religion of the here-and-now. Christianity is a religion of the hereafter. To them what happens after you're dead is more important than when you are alive." After seeing Rosen's perplexed face, he added, "When it comes to the hereafter, no one ever came back to tell us what it was like."

Rosen held his tongue. He wanted to say, "But that's what Ceil keeps telling me — that Jesus did come back from the dead. She really believes it, and she's a sensible person." He knew that everything the rabbi had said would do nothing to convince her she was wrong. Rosen didn't believe like his wife, and the rabbi's arguments were not even convincing him. So he left the conversation dissatisfied.

Within months, Rosen discovered that faith is a gift from God and believes in what cannot be understood. He surprised himself when he confessed belief in Jesus as the Messiah who was crucified for our sin and rose victorious on Easter. He didn't necessarily understand it, but the same power that raised Jesus from the dead was at work in his life. The hardness of the stone couldn't keep Jesus in the grave, and the hardness of Rosen's heart couldn't keep Jesus out. He believed that Jesus was the Messiah who came to save by overcoming death.

Easter 2
1 Peter 1:3-9

Out Of Africa

> *In this you rejoice, even if now for a little while you have had to suffer various trials, so that the genuineness of your faith — being more precious than gold that, though perishable, is tested by fire — may be found to result in praise and glory and honor when Jesus Christ is revealed. (vv. 6-7)*

A king in Africa had a close friend whom he had known since the two were boys. The friend had a habit of looking at every situation in his life and remarking, "This is good!" It didn't matter if the event was positive or negative. He always saw it as a positive.

One day the king and his lifelong friend were on a hunting expedition. The friend was in charge of loading and preparing the guns for the king. Apparently he had accidentally prepared one of the guns incorrectly. After taking the gun from his friend, the king fired it and blew off his thumb. His friend took his usual viewpoint and exclaimed, "This is good!" To which the king replied, "No, this is *not* good!" He then ordered his friend to be thrown in prison.

About a year later, the king was hunting in an area that was inhabited by cannibals. He knew better than to hunt there. Sure enough, cannibals captured him and took him to their village. They tied his hands, stacked some wood, set up a stake, and bound him to it. As they came near to set fire to the wood, they noticed that the king was missing a thumb. They were highly superstitious and never ate anyone who was less than whole. So, they untied the king and sent him on his way.

He felt fortunate as he journeyed home. He recalled the hunting incident that had taken his thumb. It seemed so unfortunate at the time, but now the king was feeling remorseful for how harshly he had treated his friend. He went immediately to the prison and had his friend released.

The king told his friend, "I had thought that it was a bad thing to lose my thumb, and I was angry that you had called it a good thing. But you were right!" He then proceeded to tell the friend all that had just happened. "Now I have come to tell you how very sorry I am for sending you to jail for so long. It was bad for me to do this."

His friend replied, "No, this is good!"

The king asked, "What do you mean, 'This is good?' How could it be good if I wrongly sent my best friend to jail for over a year?"

The friend replied, "Well, if I had not been in jail, I probably would have been hunting with you today. I am not missing any fingers. The cannibals would not have let me go."

Easter 3
Luke 24:13-35

Shocked From Recognition

Now on that same day two of them were going to a village called Emmaus, about seven miles from Jerusalem, and talking with each other about all these things that had happened. While they were talking and discussing, Jesus himself came near and went with them, but their eyes were kept from recognizing him. (vv. 13-16)

The movie *October Sky* is based on the true story of the life of Homer Hickam. The story begins with Homer as a high school student in 1957 who wants out of his small West Virginia town. The life of the entire community revolves around the local coal mine. His father works at the coal mine as do most of his friends' fathers. He fears that if he doesn't leave town after graduation he, too, will have no option other than to be a coal miner.

One evening, Homer looks up into the dark sky and witnesses an incredible sight — the Soviet satellite *Sputnik* streaked through the vast expanse of space. He develops an insatiable desire to learn more about rockets. Suddenly, he sees a way out of the coal mines. If he could get a scholarship, he could go to college and study rockets. With the encouragement of his high school science teacher, he begins to study the work of Dr. Wernher von Braun — a German-born American rocket engineer. Dr. von Braun becomes his inspiration and idol. He even writes a letter to Dr. von Braun. The scientist sends Homer an autographed picture, which becomes a cherished possession.

With enthusiasm, Homer recruits three friends to work with him in designing and building a model rocket. The boys test several metals for constructing the rocket as well as various methods of propulsion. After many failed attempts, they finally develop a functional rocket. They enter the model rocket in the county science fair.

To the elation and surprise of the boys, they win first place at the science fair. Part of the spoils of winning is a trip to the national competition in Indianapolis. However, there is one catch. Because of limited funds, only one of the boys will be allowed to go to the national science fair. The other boys choose Homer to attend since it was his initial dream and vision that gave birth to their rocket.

At the national competition, Homer wins first place. He is astonished as he hears his name called. In a stunned stupor, he walks to the podium to accept the award. He his still in a stupor as he walks back to his seat. He is dazed and confused as college recruiters are offering him scholarships. Homer barely notices their presence.

Then Homer is congratulated by a very distinguished-looking man but doesn't really seem to be aware of the conversation. Another man asks about the conversation Homer had with the distinguished-looking gentleman. Homer awakens from his shock, but has no idea who the man was or what he said. The biggest shock of all was that Homer hadn't even realized that the man who had congratulated him was none other than Dr. Wernher von Braun — the rocket engineer who had been his inspiration. Young Homer was in such shock, he hadn't recognized his idol when he spoke to him.

Could it be that the disciples on the road to Emmaus were in such shock that they didn't recognize their own leader?

Calling By Name

"The one who enters by the gate is the shepherd of the sheep. The gatekeeper opens the gate for him, and the sheep hear his voice. He calls his own sheep by name and leads them out. When he has brought out all his own, he goes ahead of them, and the sheep follow him because they know his voice." (vv. 2-4)

In the Disney movie, *Monsters, Inc.,* the truth of the lives of monsters is revealed. Monsters are in the business of scaring children because it is their business. It's their job. In a parallel world to our own, monsters tote their lunches and punch a time card while they work at a factory called Monsters, Inc. The factory contains thousands of doors that lead to the back of children's bedroom closets in our world. Doors are brought to the monsters on conveyor belts so that the monsters can simply walk into the bedrooms of children to scare them.

The monsters are ultimately harmless. In their world they are fuzzy and lovable creatures merely trying to make a living. The only reason they scare children is to capture the energy contained in their screams. Their entire world operates on this energy — much like our electricity and gas. The monsters capture the screams and compress them into a tank similar to an air tank. One of the main characters is Sully, and the plot centers on his quest to have the highest production of capturing screams.

The movie reveals the greatest secret of the monster world. While children are afraid of the monsters, the monsters are even more afraid of the children. Outside of the process of retrieving screams, the monsters want nothing to do with children. They would never touch a child for fear of contamination. In fact, they don't want to come in contact with anything a child has touched. If a monster so much as touches a child's sock, he must go through an extensive decontamination process.

A key development in the movie occurs when a little girl accidentally enters the monster world through the door in the back of her closet. Sully went to her bedroom to capture her scream but botches the job. She jumps on his back and clings to him as he returns to Monsters, Inc. After Sully discovers the toddler, he is terrified because he had been taught to fear children. He cannot return her until he finds the correct door to her room. In the meantime, he begins to take care of her. In the process, he slowly overcomes his fear. Sully actually begins to like the little girl.

And then, after a while, Sully decides to give the child a name, Boo. This is of great concern to Sully's best friend, Mike, who also works at Monsters, Inc. When Mike hears Sully has named the girl, he exclaims, "*Oh, no! Not a name! When you give it a name, that's when you get attached to it!*"

Yes, a name carries an attachment. Isn't it wonderful that Jesus, as our shepherd, knows each of our names? He is attached to us and cares for us like no one else.

Easter 5
John 14:1-14

Ice Cream In Heaven

"Do not let your hearts be troubled. Believe in God, believe also in me. In my Father's house there are many dwelling places. If it were not so, would I have told you that I go to prepare a place for you? And if I go and prepare a place for you, I will come again and will take you to myself, so that where I am, there you may be also." (vv. 1-3)

This past week marked the one-year anniversary of my mother's death. For a year now, I've been planning to write something about the week of her passing. I guess in many ways I've been avoiding it. How could I possibly sum up the life of the most influential woman in my own life? I can't. So instead I focus on her new life.

My family discovered my mother's cancer in July, and she passed away in August. We hardly had enough time to deal with the fact that she had cancer before we were dealing with death. Since she was only 66, we hadn't really even considered that death was looming. I say, "we" meaning my father and seven brothers and sisters. Personally, I had. Before my mother passed away, I had performed 36 funerals. With each funeral, I was reminded that one day I would be on the other side. One day I would grieve as my parents passed away. I wouldn't be the minister. I would be the family. However, thinking about it and being ready for it are two different things.

On Sunday afternoon, we received the call that mom had taken a turn for the worse. Not knowing what the week would hold, I went to my office and prepared for the next week's service. I quickly wrote a sermon, chose the hymns, and selected the call to worship. I wanted to be prepared to stay the week and still be ready to come home for the next Sunday's service. On Monday morning, we drove the four hours to the hospital. As we visited Mom after arriving, it was painfully obvious she was slowly slipping away.

She wasn't really eating at this point. Her main nourishment came through the IV tube. A nurse came in and offered some ice cream. Mom struggled to say, "We like ice cream." It was an understatement. I remember summers as a kid. It may just be nostalgia, but I remember making homemade ice cream *every* Saturday night. We each took turns cranking the old puke-teal '60s model ice cream freezer. If you didn't crank, you didn't eat. Dad always joked about Mom's love of ice cream, saying that she could sit naked in an eight-foot snow bank and eat an entire gallon of ice cream. Yeah, Mom loved ice cream. Ironically, "We like ice cream," turned out to be the last words she spoke. It was very fitting.

She held on through Tuesday barely breathing and too weak to speak. You could literally see the life draining out of her as her eyes began to sink back. My brothers and sisters and I gathered around her on Tuesday evening. Recognizing that the quality of life was no longer a reality, we tried to comfort her. We all said our good-byes and told her it was okay to pass on to a better life in heaven. Being raised as preacher's kids, we all were strong in faith and comfortable with her life continuing in Christ. Finally, at 3:50 Wednesday morning, Mom took her last breath. I had just come into the room about five minutes beforehand to take my shift of staying with her. I considered it a privilege to have been present with my mother as she went to heaven.

For years I have been disappointed with Christians who fail to see the joy of death. I don't dispute the need to grieve, because it is both natural and necessary. When we lose someone we love, it hurts. But to grieve without having hope in eternal life is not Christian. We have hope because Jesus has promised us that death is not the end of life but only a transition to a new life. We grieve for our loss, not the loss of our family member or friend. Our loss is their gain.

But now, as death became personal, my theology was being tested. Mom's funeral was on Saturday of that week. After my preparations from the previous Sunday, I was back preaching at my church the day after the funeral. One of the church members asked me how I could preach the day following my mother's funeral. How could I not? What better place to be than church? What better task to do than preach? Mom brought me up in the faith. She would certainly want me to live and express that faith she had taught me. Besides, I had been with death all week. It was now time to live. It was time to live my life while Mom lived her new life.

After Mom passed early that Wednesday morning, my family was still sitting in the hospital waiting room where we had camped out over the past three and a half days. We were still in shock and half asleep as we were trying to figure out the next step. As we were talking, I suggested we go to the local Braum's Ice Cream store and order a Butterfinger Mix in Mom's honor. A Butterfinger Mix from Braum's was her all-time favorite. We all laughed. We could laugh because we knew we did have something to celebrate. Mom was no longer suffering and probably eating ice cream in heaven. Since it tastes so heavenly on earth, I can only imagine what it tastes like there in the sweetest of places.

So here it is a year later. It's actually three days after the anniversary of my mother's entrance to heavenly life. I'm finally writing my thoughts. What finally forced me to sit down and write this? Well, my church had an ice cream social yesterday. Not that you don't already know it, Mom, but I made your favorite — Butterfinger. And it was good — as sweet as saving grace.

Easter 6
1 Peter 3:13-22

The Legend Of Thud

Now who will harm you if you are eager to do what is good? But even if you do suffer for doing what is right, you are blessed. Do not fear what they fear and do not be intimidated, but in your hearts sanctify Christ as Lord. (vv. 13-15a)

There was a little rabbit that lived near a tall palm tree. One day a coconut fell from the palm tree and landed right behind the rabbit. The coconut hit the ground with a loud thud.

The noise surprised and frightened the little bunny so much that he took off running. He was so scared that he never looked back to see what had created the noise. An antelope saw him running and asked, "Rabbit, why are you running so fast?"

Rabbit shouted, "Thud is coming!"

Antelope didn't know who or what Thud was, but also didn't want to find out. She started running, too. Just then, Rabbit and Antelope scampered past Warthog. He called out to them, "Why are you running?"

"Thud is coming!" yelled Antelope.

"Run for your life!" added Rabbit.

Warthog started running as fast as his short little legs could gallop. Before long they all passed a panda. Panda starting jogging with Warthog and asked, "Why are all the animals running?"

Warthog snorted, "Thud is coming!" Panda joined the exodus.

Before long, all the animals were stampeding out of the forest as they wailed about the terrible Thud chasing after them. Finally the herd of alarmed animals came toward a lion. Feeling somewhat safe with Lion and needing to catch their breath, they stopped. Lion asked, "Why are you running?"

As if given a cue, they roared in unison, "Because Thud is coming!"

Lion asked, "And who, pray tell, is Thud?"

Panda looked at Warthog. Warthog looked at Antelope. And Antelope looked at Rabbit. Rabbit finally spoke, "I don't know for sure. I didn't see him. I only heard him!"

Lion asked "Well, then where does Thud live?"

Rabbit answered, "Back by the coconut grove."

Then Lion started walking toward the coconut grove. The rest of the animals crept a safe distance behind — but not too far lest they lose their protection. When they made it to the palm trees, Lion told the rest of the animals to watch and listen. A moment later, a coconut fell from a tall palm tree. They watched it fall, and heard the end result — a loud thud as it hit the ground.

Lion very smartly said, "There is your terrible Thud. You have been scared of a coconut."

The Ascension Of Our Lord
Ephesians 1:15-23

We Have The Majority

God put this power to work in Christ when he raised him from the dead and seated him at his right hand in the heavenly places, far above all rule and authority and power and dominion, and above every name that is named, not only in this age but also in the age to come. And he has put all things under his feet and has made him the head over all things for the church, which is his body, the fullness of him who fills all in all. (vv. 20-23)

A new minister was having trouble with her congregation; they couldn't agree on anything. The chairman of the church board said, "Preacher, this can't continue. There has to be a meeting, and we have to settle our differences once and for all." The minister agreed.

The time for the meeting arrived. The minister, the chairman of the board, and all ten board members met around a beautiful oak table in the conference room of the church. One by one the issues were dealt with and on each issue, it became more and more apparent that everything the minister said went in one ear and out the other. The church board chair said, "Come on, Preacher, enough of this. Let's put it to a vote and allow the majority to rule." Then he passed out slips of paper to each board member. They all voted, and turned in their pieces of paper. After the votes were counted, the chairman said, "You can count them yourself, Preacher, if you want, but it's eleven to one against you. We have the majority."

The minister was upset by the way things had been handled. She stood up and stated, "Just because you're all in agreement, you think that you're right and I'm wrong. A vote doesn't make this God's will." Then she imposingly raised her arms while looking heavenward and said, "I call upon our Great and Loving God to give us a sign that I'm right and you're wrong."

No sooner these words left her lips than a ferocious clap of thunder was heard followed by a radiant flash of lightning that struck the oak table and split it in two. The room was overflowing with a hazy smoke and the smell of charred wood. The chairman and the rest of the board were all cowering on the floor amidst the debris. And yet, the minister still stood, untouched, in the same spot where she had just called for a sign from God. Ever so slowly, the board chair lifted himself out of the wreckage. His hair was scorched, his glasses were hanging from one ear, and his clothing was disorderly. While still trying to catch his breath he said, "All right, eleven to two. But we still have the majority."

Easter 7
1 Peter 4:12-14; 5:6-11

Blessing Or Bane?

> *And after you have suffered for a little while, the God of grace, who has called you to his eternal glory in Christ, will himself restore, strengthen, and establish you. (v. 10)*

Long ago, there was a poor old woman who lived with her only son near China's northern border. One night their only horse wandered away. All the neighbors came to them and said they were sorry that this terrible thing happened to them. The old woman replied, "How do you know it's terrible? Perhaps this will soon turn out to be a blessing."

A few months later, the horse returned with a whole herd of wild horses. The neighbors helped them put the horses into a corral and congratulated them at their good luck. The old woman replied, "How do you know it's good luck? Perhaps this will soon turn out to be a cause of misfortune."

Sure enough, a week later the boy tried to ride one of the wild horses. The horse bucked him off and the son broke his thighbone in the fall. The neighbors soon heard about it and said, "What bad luck!" The old woman responded, "How do you know it's bad luck? Perhaps this will soon turn out to be a blessing."

Well, soon after that the northern tribes started a big invasion of the border regions. A Chinese warlord rode into town with his army to recruit every man and boy in town to fight in the war. All able-bodied young men took up arms and fought against the invaders. When he saw that the old woman's son had a broken leg, the warlord left him in the town and rode away.

The fighting was very lethal. As a result, ninety percent of the men in the border region died. But the old woman's son was spared.

He had not joined in the fighting because of his injury. And once again, the neighbors came and rejoiced in his good luck.

Things that seem unfair when they happen to us sometimes turn out to help us. What may appear to be suffering, may be something that God uses as a benefit.

The Day Of Pentecost
Acts 2:1-21

It Only Takes A Spark

When the day of Pentecost had come, they were all together in one place. And suddenly from heaven there came a sound like the rush of a violent wind, and it filled the entire house where they were sitting. Divided tongues, as of fire, appeared among them, and a tongue rested on each of them. (vv. 1-3)

Several years ago, God lit a match under me and led me to volunteer as a junior high counselor for my denomination's summer camp. I'd done a little youth ministry work before, but nothing could have prepared me for that week.

Our curriculum for the camp focused on the Christian liturgical year. We wanted youth to understand better the church's worship cycle and connect it with their faith.

As was expected, the week was very inspirational. Everything went along as planned — until the final evening. That night was Advent according to our curriculum. We worshiped in an open-air tabernacle and had an Advent wreath in the front on a small wooden utility table.

To close the service, we lit the wreath's candles. We watched the flames flicker as we held hands, formed a circle, and sang a closing song. Emotions ran high with the anticipation of the coming Christ-child and with our departure from camp the next day.

It was our group's tradition to end each camp with a bonfire, so our circle of worshipers became a straight line as we silently walked hand-in-hand out of the tabernacle. The bonfire was at the end of a canyon about 300 wooded yards away, and we headed there in a spirit of worship.

As usual, tears flowed while we burned 3 x 5 cards containing messages to God. Afterward, as we walked back to the main part of the camp, I spotted the two senior high camp's deans in front of the tabernacle. They looked like parents waiting for a curfew breaking teenager to pull into the driveway. The look in their eyes could have melted plastic.

As I got closer, I understood why. The table that had held the Advent wreath was black, and the wreath was an unrecognizable circular glob. A radio and a slide projector for sing-along slides were also on the table. At least that's what they used to be.

My first thought — maybe a hopeful prayer — was that it was a very elaborate practical joke. But then I looked at the rafters five feet above the table. They were charred and burned halfway through.

Yes, in the midst of a highly emotional and inspirational worship service, no one blew out the Advent candles. The candles burned down, the wreath and table caught on fire, and the boombox and slide projector melted.

Luckily, the senior high deans played firefighters before any more damage was done. Everything on the table was destroyed except for two items that were untouched. The first was a copy of the camp curriculum. The table was charred up to the book.

The other item was a sing-along slide. When we removed it from the deformed carriage, we held it up to the light to read it. It was from the song "Pass It On," and it read, "It only takes a spark." We knew that.

Come, Thou Almighty King

The grace of the Lord Jesus Christ, the love of God, and the communion of the Holy Spirit be with all of you. (v. 13)

Around 1745, during the American Revolution, a detachment of British soldiers burst into a church in a Long Island congregation startling the unsuspecting worshipers. The commanding officer demanded that the frightened congregation sing the British national hymn, "God Save Our Gracious King." The congregation simultaneously sang the right tune — what we know as "America" or "My Country 'Tis of Thee." But instead of singing lyrics praising the King of England, they sang praises to the Trinitarian God — Father, Son, and Holy Spirit. The lyrics they sang were the hymn "Come, Thou Almighty King":

Come, thou almighty King,
help us thy name to sing,
help us to praise!
Father all glorious,
o'er all victorious,
come and reign over us,
Ancient of Days!

That is one legend of the origin of the hymn. The hymn has also been attributed to Charles Wesley, but this is not known for sure since it was published anonymously. The theory goes that Wesley wrote the hymn as an imitation of the new British national anthem. It was his way of refocusing people on God's kingdom instead of an earthly kingdom. As the theory goes, Wesley intentionally did not lay claim to writing the lyrics since the new lyrics were a rebellion against words of the royal hymn. This theory is plausible since the hymn first appeared in George Whitefield's *Collection of Hymns for Social Worship* published in 1757. Whitefield was a good friend and protégé of Wesley.

Over the years, the song was sung to the "America" tune and also to the tune "Italian Hymn" with both tunes being used for the same time period. Eventually, the tune "America" became one of our national anthems and the "Italian Hymn" tune became permanently wedded with "Come, Thou Almighty King."

No matter what the origin, the song is inexplicably tied to Trinity Sunday because of the content of the lyrics — a triumphant praise to the triune God: Father and King, Incarnate Word, and Holy Comforter. As one verse says:

To thee, great One in Three,
eternal praises be,
hence evermore.
Thy sovereign majesty
may we in glory see,
and to eternity
love and adore.

Proper 4 / Pentecost 2 / Ordinary Time 9
Romans 1:16-17; 3:22b-28 (29-31)

Grace For All

For there is no distinction, since all have sinned and fall short of the glory of God; they are now justified by his grace as a gift, through the redemption that is in Christ Jesus. (vv. 22b-24)

She was young, but already she had a past. Alcohol. Drugs. Sexual promiscuity. She was heavily involved in partying. However, there was a church in her neighborhood that she passed frequently. One Sunday, she felt a deep urging from within her to attend worship. She did and discovered the urging came from God. She went back the next Sunday. The worship gave her a sense of peace. She eventually responded by professing her faith that Jesus was God's Son sent to reclaim her as a lost child. In faith, she started turning her life around and became a new creation in Christ.

As time went on, she became even more involved in the church. She eventually started working within the children's ministry. Her inner beauty was beginning to catch up to her already existing outer beauty. She caught the eye of the minister's son. His heart soon followed. They became inseparable and it was apparent where the relationship was headed. They began to make wedding plans.

However, the bliss of young lovers soon encountered the problems of hypocritical thinking. About one half of the church did not think it was appropriate for the minister's son to marry someone whose past included drugs and partying. They had held their collective tongue while the two dated, hoping it was just a passing relationship. But now with a wedding being planned, they spoke out. Conversations concerning the matter occurred before meetings and in the parking lot after services. To avoid a split, a meeting was called so that everyone could express his or her opinions openly and honestly.

Some were a little too honest. Many were not tactful. One woman said, "That woman gives a bad image to our church. She's not good enough to be a part of us, let alone marry the minister's son!" A man added, "She's like Bathsheba exposing herself in front of King David. She's nothing but a temptress!" The tension increased as the meeting was getting out of hand. The young woman burst into tears as her past was being dredged up like a long forgotten sunken ship.

The minister's son couldn't stand to see his future wife tormented any longer. He interrupted the madness and said, "Do you hear what you are saying? My fiancée's past is not what is on trial here. What you are really trying is the power of God's grace and forgiveness. You debate whether or not God has the ability to forgive a shameful past. You question whether or not God loves us enough to save us from our sin. Do you really believe that God doesn't love us enough to forgive us of our past when we have repented?"

All the people present began to weep as their hearts were opened to the truth spoken by the minister's son. They realized that they had been doubting God's ability to reclaim a lost soul. With new eyes, they saw the purpose of Christ's death and resurrection.

Too often we forget that God's promise of redemption is offered to all regardless of the magnitude of their failures. We are all in the same boat. The good news is that forgiveness is available to all who profess and believe — the hypocrite as well as the immoral.

Proper 5 / Pentecost 3 / Ordinary Time 10
Matthew 9:9-13, 18-26

Fruit Punch, A Poppy Seed Muffin, And A Bar

And as he sat at dinner in the house, many tax collectors and sinners came and were sitting with him and his disciples. When the Pharisees saw this, they said to his disciples, "Why does your teacher eat with tax collectors and other sinners?" But when he heard this, he said, "Those who are well have no need of a physician, but those who are sick. Go and learn what this means, 'I desire mercy, not sacrifice.' For I have come to call not the righteous but sinners." (vv. 10-13)

Kirk is a good friend of mine. Both he and his wife have served churches as youth ministers. Now they own their own business, but because of their love for youth and ministry, they volunteer as sponsors for the youth group at their church.

I was honored when Kirk asked me to serve as worship leader on a trip his youth group was taking. All expenses paid? Great. Destination? Colorado for skiing — even better. Now some of you are saying I lucked out, but be honest, you're secretly wishing you had an offer for a free ski trip. Others are saying, "Yeah right, a worship leader for a ski trip. What do you do — give a five minute devotion and hit the slopes?"

Well, this was a ski retreat — not a ski trip. This is not mere semantics. We spent an hour every morning in worship before we went skiing. In the evenings, we had a thirty-minute close-the-day worship service. Both times involved singing, story-preaching, sharing, praying, communion, and challenging each other. My friend Kirk had done this before. The skiing is merely a draw to get the youth to go on a retreat and encounter God.

We drove all night and into the next afternoon to Glenwood Springs. After a late lunch, we checked into the Hotel Colorado. (Anyone else have a slight variation of an old Eagles' tune running through your head now?) Other than falling down on the slopes, the one thing I hate more than anything about a ski trip is driving all night. I didn't drive that much, but I was tired. After all, the copilot has to keep the pilot awake. Anyway, starting the retreat with sleep deprivation was not a good sign for worship. After checking in my luggage, I immediately began setting up our worship area.

The worship area was a hotel conference room — the seating and furniture arrangement didn't lend itself to worship. So I began a transformation project. I moved tables — folding and leaning some while repositioning others. I set up the sound system and overhead projector. I tuned my guitar and set up its stand. I took one table and created a makeshift altar complete with chalice and plate. Other, more personal symbols would be added by the youth during the service. At last, everything was in place.

At 9:00 p.m. we herded the youth to the room. As we started to enter the conference room, we discovered the room was double-booked. It seems there was another youth group from our same hometown staying at the Hotel Colorado. Someone had confused the two groups. We decided that by juggling our times, we could share the room for the evening. But this was only a temporary arrangement. The other group needed the room primarily for breakfast. The set up they needed for the room was so vastly different that we would constantly be moving tables and equipment. The hotel offered us another conference room.

After that was all straightened out, we had our worship service which included communion. Somehow our wires were crossed, and we didn't have bread or grape juice available. It was now approaching 10:00 p.m. and the only thing we could get in the hotel was a packet of fruit punch and a poppy seed muffin! Not exactly traditional, but it provided a teaching moment. I explained that at the original Last Supper Jesus used regular ordinary table food — bread and wine. The elements were holy only because they were to represent Jesus. Likewise, our ordinary poppy seed muffin and fruit punch were holy because they caused us to remember Jesus and his importance in our lives. It was a pretty good cover and theologically sound, but it was also a reminder that things were not going as planned.

The next day, I got up early to set up our worship area once again — in the new conference room. Up went the sound system, overhead projector, guitar, and altar. The room wasn't as good as the first, but we could make do. A trip to the local Wal-Mart provided us with real bread and grape juice. Things were looking up!

But then we noticed every time we went into our worship area, all of our stuff had been rearranged. After skiing all day, I had to recreate the worship area. But the kicker came when we were gathering to leave the hotel for dinner and a hotel staff person rolled by a luggage cart containing all of our worship stuff! It seems we now had a conflict with the second room. It was no longer available. After a conversation with the events coordinator, we decided the only available room for our worship service the next morning was the hotel bar. Since our worship was at 8:00 a.m., the bar would be closed. So that is exactly where we worshiped.

As strange as it may sound, it was fitting. If Jesus were humanly alive today, he would take an ordinary bar and make it holy — kind of like bread and wine or fruit punch and poppy seed muffins. He wouldn't be judgmental about the regular use of the room; he would simply talk about a new creation. He would talk about how life can be better. He would challenge us to move beyond stereotypes and judgment. After all, Jesus was known to consort with tax collectors, prostitutes, and other riffraff.

So we worshiped in a bar. All eighteen of us — and an occasional curious onlooker who peeked in and wondered what was going on in a bar at 8:00 in the morning. Were they looking for the breakfast buffet? Or did the sound of a group of youth singing about their faith stir their soul and draw them in? Who knows? Maybe someone hoping to have a sip of Jack Daniels, took a sip of Jesus Christ instead.

Proper 6 / Pentecost 4 / Ordinary Time 11
Romans 5:1-8

From Suffering To Hope

And not only that, but we also boast in our sufferings, knowing that suffering produces endurance, and endurance produces character, and character produces hope, and hope does not disappoint us, because God's love has been poured into our hearts through the Holy Spirit that has been given to us. (vv. 3-5)

For nearly a year, Lee had been working at a church as their part-time youth minister. He was a senior in college and would graduate in a month. He had started the youth ministry basically from nothing. There were six youth when he began and now there were about fifteen. There was still untapped potential within the group. Lee really wanted to continue working with this church, but would need full-time employment upon graduation.

Lee related to the Education Committee within the church. He approached that committee with the idea to hire him full-time for the summer so that the group could increase their activities. They could plan more trips and attend camps. Lee had been raised in a different denomination than this church, so he asked the committee if they were the appropriate people to discuss the proposal. The committee assured Lee they had the authority. They had additional funds to raise the salary and authorized the change in status. They were all hopeful that things would work out over the summer, and Lee could be hired on a full-time basis throughout the year.

An announcement was made in the church newsletter, and Lee began holding regular office hours beginning in May. After a month and a half of working full-time, the Senior Minister, Robert, called Lee into his office. He had just discovered that Lee had been hired full-time. He demanded an explanation for all the secrecy.

The truth was there was no secrecy on Lee's part. His mistake was assuming that the Education Committee had communicated with Robert. Robert delegated responsibility to committee chairs and did not attend their meetings. There was a power struggle in the church between the Education chair and Robert, so Robert wasn't ever told of the Education Committee's decision. Lee was caught in the middle. To further complicate things, Robert did not hold regular office hours at church. He chose instead to work mainly from his home office. Consequently, he was not aware that Lee was in the office every day.

Robert told Lee that he would immediately be placed back on part-time salary. There were some in the church who thought the "extra" salary that Lee was paid during the month and a half of full-time status should be repaid. Lee was devastated. He felt he had done nothing wrong as he tried to go through proper channels. He indicated to Robert that on the basis of working full-time he had made purchases and signed a lease for an apartment. He was unsure how he would cover his bills. Robert replied, "That's not my problem."

Lee found it stressful to be at church. He found another part-time job to cover his expenses. With his time now committed to this job as well, he had to cancel the weeklong trips and camps. Robert accused him of doing it for spite. This made the already poor relationship between the two that much more tenuous.

Lee felt confused, angry, and helpless. All he knew to do was pray. God became his refuge and his shelter. Lee began searching for a full-time youth ministry job within his own denomination. By the end of the summer, he was hired on a full-time basis at another church where he stayed for four years. Lee made it through the suffering and learned through the process. The Holy Spirit guided him to character and gave him a hope that did not disappoint.

Proper 7 / Pentecost 5 / Ordinary 12
Matthew 10:24-39

How Insignificant?

Are not two sparrows sold for a penny? Yet not one of them will fall to the ground apart from your Father. And even the hairs of your head are all counted. So do not be afraid; you are of more value than many sparrows. (vv. 29-31)

I stood in line with my wife to check our bags at the airport in Charleston, South Carolina. We were completing our vacation by beginning the long journey home. We were using frequent flyer miles, so we had layovers in Charlotte, North Carolina, and Dallas-Forth Worth before arriving in Fort Smith, Arkansas.

The attendant at the U.S. Air counter asked, "What's your final destination?" We replied, "Fort Smith, Arkansas."

She responded, "I think that's a first. I've never sent anyone there." We explained that it was a small airport — only two gates. We didn't tell her, but the airport was so small, our pilot also collected our boarding passes before take-off.

I tried to draw her a mental picture and said, "It's about the same size as the airport in Fayetteville." With the University of Arkansas in Fayetteville, I thought she would connect.

She responded, "Is that in Arkansas?"

I concluded that Fort Smith and Fayetteville were insignificant in her life. When one lives in Heavener, Oklahoma, Fort Smith is the big city. It has a mall. That makes it big for all the small towns surrounding Fort Smith. It became apparent to me that Fort Smith is not big when you are from New York, L. A., or even Charleston.

We landed in DFW to connect with our little American Eagle prop plane to fly us to Fort Smith. To get to the plane, we had to take a shuttle bus from the terminal to the runway. After they announced our flight, we got on the bus and waited for everyone else to board as well. A few minutes later, a man of gigantic proportions — about seven feet tall — stepped into the bus. He was too tall to stand on the bus. He was hunched over with his head bent down as he put his bags on the luggage rack.

I had immediate visions of our prop plane, which I affectionately called a crop duster. I leaned over to my wife and said, "Man, that guy's going to be in a world of hurt on the plane!"

The giant raised his head to find a seat, and moved to the back of the bus to sit with a woman and a small boy, apparently his family. They were only three seats away, which caused me to say a quick prayer that my previous comment was not overheard. A gentleman in between the giant and me shook hands with the giant. His hand appeared miniaturized in the process. He said something like, "I enjoy your work." The giant nodded without really saying anything.

Suddenly, it clicked with me. The big guy on the shuttle bus was Bryant "Big Country" Reeves, the starting center for the Vancouver Grizzlies. An NBA star was one of 35 people flying on my prop plane to little insignificant Fort Smith, Arkansas. Why? Because he grew up in tinier and even more insignificant Gans, Oklahoma. He was going home to see his parents.

At the beginning of the day, Fort Smith was put in perspective for me. Small. Insignificant. At the end of the day, that perspective was reversed. Fort Smith was a key element in getting "Big Country" home. Like beauty, importance is in the eye of the beholder.

It was a reminder that even when we start feeling small and unimportant in life, we are still significant and important to God. God knows everything about us, including the hairs on our head. No one is insignificant no matter what others may say. In God's eyes, we have great worth.

Proper 8 / Pentecost 6 / Ordinary Time 13
Matthew 10:40-42

King Thrushbeard

Whoever welcomes you welcomes me, and whoever welcomes me welcomes the one who sent me. (v. 40)

A Brothers Grimm fairy tale tells of a king who had a beautiful daughter. However, she was also so proud and arrogant that she felt no suitor was good enough for her. Once the king made a great feast and invited all the young eligible bachelors from far and wide. They were all assembled in a row according to their rank and standing. Then the king's daughter was led through the ranks, but to every one she had some objection to make. One was too fat. Another was too tall. The third was too short. The fourth was too pale. The fifth too red. The sixth was not straight enough. So she had something rude to say against every one. She was particularly cruel to a good king whose chin had grown a little crooked. She laughed, "He has a chin like a thrush's beak!" and she nicknamed him King Thrushbeard.

Her father was not pleased that she did nothing but mock all the suitors. He was very angry, and swore to marry her to the first beggar that came to his doors. A few days later a fiddler dressed in dirty, ragged clothes came and sang beneath the palace windows. The king invited him into the palace where he sang before the king and his daughter. When he had ended, he took off his hat to collect a meager gift. The king said, "Your song has pleased me so well that I will give you my daughter to be your wife." The king's daughter shuddered, but the king said, "I have taken an oath, and I will keep it." The priest came, and immediately married them.

The king then sent his daughter away with her beggar husband. As they were walking, they came to a large forest and she asked, "To whom does that beautiful forest belong?" The beggar replied, "It belongs to King Thrushbeard; if you had taken him, it would have been yours." She suddenly regretted her rejection of King Thrushbeard.

Then they came to a meadow, and she asked, "To whom does this beautiful green meadow belong?" Her husband responded, "It belongs to King Thrushbeard; if you had taken him, it would have been yours." Again, she regretted rejecting Thrushbeard.

Next they came to a large town, and she asked again, "To whom does this fine large town belong?" The fiddler sang, "It belongs to King Thrushbeard; if you had taken him, it would have been yours." She was in misery.

Her misery only worsened when they arrived at a little hut. She said, "Oh, goodness! What a small house! To whom does this miserable, mean shack belong?" The fiddler answered, "That is my house and yours, where we shall live together."

She had to stoop to enter. Then she realized the reality of her new life. There were no servants. Not only did she have to do for herself, but also she had to do for her husband. After she cooked a sparse meal, with her husband teaching her, they went to bed. Her husband woke her early the next day to tend the house.

A few days later, they ran out of food, so the husband put his wife to work weaving baskets and spinning thread. Her hands were too delicate for such work. He then sent her to work selling pots and earthenware in the market place. She was very afraid of being seen and recognized by the people of her father's kingdom, but hunger drove her to comply. At first she succeeded. She was still beautiful, which attracted a crowd. However, one day, when she was selling a large amount of new crockery, a drunken cavalry man came galloping along and trampled the pots.

As a last resort, the husband sent her to his king's palace to work in the kitchen. She did the dirtiest work just to be paid in the scraps from the king's table. She had a little jar in her two pockets to keep the scraps.

Before long, the king's eldest son was celebrating his wedding. The former princess went to the hall catch a glimpse of her former life. The decorations and the people were all beautiful. She was saddened, and cursed the pride and arrogance that had tumbled her to poverty. She smelled the delicious dishes being served. She looked forward to eating the scraps from her take-home jars.

All at once the king's son entered, greatly adorned, wearing velvet, silk, and gold. It was King Thrushbeard, and when he saw the beautiful former princess standing by the door, he asked her to dance. She was afraid he would recognize her and tried to refuse. He insisted. As he led her, the string by which her pockets were hung broke. The jars fell down. The soup ran out, and the scraps were scattered all about. Everyone stared and laughed.

The princess was mortified, and she turned to run. But King Thrushbeard would not let her go. He said tenderly, "Do not be afraid, the fiddler who has been living with you in that wretched shanty and I are one. For love of you I disguised myself so; and I also was the cavalryman who rode through your crockery. This was all done to humble your proud spirit."

Then she wept bitterly and said, "I have done great wrong, and am not worthy to be your wife."

But he said, "Be comforted, the evil days are past; now we will celebrate our wedding." Then the maids-in-waiting came and put on her the most splendid clothing. Her father and his whole court came and wished her happiness in her marriage with King Thrushbeard. True joy and happiness were finally discovered as they lived happily ever after.

Proper 9 / Pentecost 7 / Ordinary Time 14
Matthew 11:16-19, 25-30

Rest For The Weary

> *"Come to me, all you that are weary and are carrying heavy burdens, and I will give you rest. Take my yoke upon you, and learn from me; for I am gentle and humble in heart, and you will find rest for your souls. For my yoke is easy, and my burden is light. (vv. 28-30)*

In June of 1988, I served as a youth director at a small Congregational church in Oklahoma City. The closest independent Congregational church was one in Joplin, Missouri. Those two churches would occasionally get together for youth events. One such event was a backpacking trip through the Ouachita National Forest in southeastern Oklahoma near the Arkansas border. My group had been backpacking in Colorado the previous year. Many of the youth felt backpacking in our home state was not very adventurous, so on this trip my group consisted only of two youth and myself. The group from Joplin was small as well — two men, a teenager, and a five-year-old boy.

The plan was a fifteen-mile, three-day hike. We would leisurely hike five miles each day and set up camp for a relaxing evening under the stars. The two men from Joplin planned the trip. They had hiked the trail in January and thought it would be a great place to take our youth groups for a challenging adventure. We all met at the trailhead, loaded our gear, and started hiking at 1:00 in the afternoon. Thirty minutes later we stopped at a stream to take a break and refill our water bottles. We used iodine pills to make the water drinkable. With full water bottles, we resumed our journey.

It was a hot day. We didn't know it at the time, but temperature records were literally being broken. As we continued to hike, we noticed something that disturbed us. Every time we approached a stream indicated on our map, there was no stream to be found. Apparently, it had been very hot for a very long time.

As we continued to pass dried up streams, we began to feel more uncomfortable. One of my youth was a twelve-year-old boy named Cory. This was his first outing with the youth group. It was also his first time to go backpacking. He was not dealing well with our declining water situation. He would plop down on a boulder and say, "I quit." I tried to explain that quitting was not an option. They didn't have cell phones then. We couldn't call Rescue 911.

We decided most of the team should go on ahead. One of the adults from Joplin stayed back with me so that we could encourage Cory to keep on hiking. This man stayed just ahead of us as he scouted out the trail. Things were looking quite bleak as we were consuming our water and not finding any streams to replenish our supply. We were starting to get very hungry, but were afraid to eat because it would only make us thirsty. So we nibbled and pressed on. To complicate matters, the dehydration was affecting me in other ways. Even though we had treated the water, the overexertion and exhaustion had given me a terrible case of River Revenge, a.k.a. diarrhea. Let me assure you, the forest is a terrible place to experience such suffering.

In the midst of this, I tried to encourage Cory. I shared with him one of my favorite scriptures, Proverbs 3:5: "Trust in the Lord and do not rely on what you think you know. Lean on him and he will make your path straight." In his twelve-year-old wisdom, Cory questioned the wisdom of the passage even as it gave him hope. Little did Cory know that I was quoting the scripture to myself as much as I was to him. At the tender age of 21, I sensed death looking over our shoulders. As darkness set in, it became harder to see the markings for the trail. With all the twists and alternative pathways, I wondered at times if we were even still on the trail.

I peered at my watch using the remaining light of dusk. It was 9:00 — eight hours after we had begun the journey. Daylight waned. I was tired. I was thirsty. I was hungry. Also, I desperately needed a real bathroom. I now had less than a quarter inch of water left in my bottle. My hope was only as strong as the daylight. Would God answer the prayers Cory and I frantically prayed?

In the dimness of dusk, I saw one of God's most beautiful creations. Water. In the distance was the rest of our group — camped next to the Kiamichi River. Water! At last; beautiful, plentiful water! We had hiked nine miles, but we had found the life-giving source we sought. I threw off my gear, ran to the river, splashed myself, and filled my water bottle. I was so hungry that I ate cold stew out of the can. I was so tired I didn't mind sleeping on rocks because now it was too dark to see where to pitch a tent.

The important thing was that we were alive. We had made it! I was weary — exhausted in body and soul. But I was being revived, and it was more than the effects of the water. I knew that the only reason we had made it was because Cory and I had worshiped along the journey. We had prayed. We had quoted scripture. We had rest time with God. We had to — there were no alternatives. We needed God.

My soul was revived. I knew God was God, and I was not. God was in control, not me. I realized that was a good thing. The weary soul had received rest. We were thankful, and we continued to worship.

Proper 10 / Pentecost 8 / Ordinary Time 15
Genesis 25:19-34

Hitting A Winner

Once when Jacob was cooking a stew, Esau came in from the field, and he was famished. Esau said to Jacob, "Let me eat some of that red stuff, for I am famished!" (Therefore he was called Edom.) Jacob said, "First sell me your birthright." Esau said, "I am about to die; of what use is a birthright to me?" Jacob said, "Swear to me first." So he swore to him, and sold his birthright to Jacob. Then Jacob gave Esau bread and lentil stew, and he ate and drank, and rose and went his way. Thus Esau despised his birthright. (vv. 29-34)

Diane Ketterling bought an old 18-by-20-inch picture frame from Outskirts Antique Shop in Chandler, Oklahoma, for $100. She planned to replace the picture in the frame with a re-sized photograph of her ancestors. She went to a local photo shop and dropped everything off to have the work done. Ketterling then left town on business.

The photo shop owner removed the picture only to discover more pictures. One of the photos about to be discarded was a picture of former President Woodrow Wilson. A closer inspection revealed that two additional photos — also believed to be of Wilson — were behind the first one in the frame. When Ketterling returned, she discovered the rare find. One photograph portrayed Wilson at about age 55. The other two photos are believed to be of Wilson at a younger age. An appraiser informed her that the rare photos could be worth as much as $100,000.

Jim Booze owns the antique shop that sold Ketterling the rare photographs. He said the frame came from an estate sale on the East Coast. He often buys a variety of items from large sales nationwide. He was not upset at her good fortune. He figures she just happened to "hit on a winner" with the purchase. Booze said, "I would have liked to come across that, but I am glad she got it. She's a real swell lady, and she has shopped with me for several years. I am sure she is appreciating it."

He has also been the beneficiary of rare finds. He said he once bought a piece of antique furniture that contained two old newspapers between the mirror and the wood. The newspapers announced the assassination of President Lincoln. Booze said they were appraised at $900 each.

He said, "Sometimes you get some; sometimes you miss some of them. It's part of the business, and I have fun with it. You just never know about things out of the past."

If she sells the photographs, Ketterling said she plans to give the photo shop owner a share of the money. Ketterling commented on the photo shop owner, "She is very fair and very honest. A lot of people would take the pictures, and I wouldn't have known anything about that. I owe a lot to her because she was honest."

Jacob was hardly that honest or fair in dealing with Esau's birthright. He sought to capitalize on his brother's weakness. He cheated him. And yet, God used Jacob in the lineage of a great nation. This speaks of God's great mercy more than God's approval of Jacob's methods.

(From a story by Michael Bratcher in the 10/11/02 *Daily Oklahoman*.)

Proper 11 / Pentecost 9 / Ordinary Time 16
Romans 8:12-25

Exodus House

So then, brothers and sisters, we are debtors, not to the flesh, to live according to the flesh — for if you live according to the flesh, you will die; but if by the Spirit you put to death the deeds of the body, you will live. For all who are led by the Spirit of God are children of God. For you did not receive a spirit of slavery to fall back into fear, but you have received a spirit of adoption. When we cry, "Abba! Father!" it is that very Spirit bearing witness with our spirit that we are children of God. (vv. 12-16)

Marilyn Cherry was not raised in a Christian home. She went to church a few times when she was younger. Her grandmother was a good woman, who sent Marilyn and her siblings on a church bus. Her limited time in church didn't make a lasting impression. She chose a harder life.

She was arrested in Texas for manufacturing methamphetamine in 1996. She had a vision her first night she was incarcerated. Perhaps nightmare is a more apt description. In her dream, a monster was chasing her through a shopping mall. He was so close, she could feel his breath on her neck. She also sensed someone running alongside her. She couldn't see who it was, but she knew he was there.

Every time she ran past a window at the mall, she could see a huge church across the street. She felt that if she could just make it there, she would be safe. The person running beside her kept fending off the monster. As she was running, she noticed that she was covered in blood — but she was not bleeding. She finally came to an open door and made it across the street. She fell exhausted on her knees at the foot of the steps, and the church doors opened up. She looked around and noticed that the monster had disappeared. Then she woke up. She knew then that Jesus was running alongside her in her dream as her protector. The blood she had seen was his, as he had given his life to spare hers.

She then started attending all the chapel services in prison. She asked questions and learned how to pray. She read all the literature that she could get her hands on. She was feeding a hunger-related spiritual starvation and was determined to turn her life around. God was leading the way.

She was released from a drug rehabilitation center in October, 2000, and went to the Salvation Army Substance Abuse Aftercare facility in Dallas, Texas. She immediately went to work at a deli. She also helped at a nearby facility that assisted the disabled in the work force.

Marilyn eventually moved to Oklahoma City, Oklahoma to live at Exodus House — an apartment ministry of the United Methodist Church for ex-convicts. She was accepted with open arms there and began to thrive. She felt loved and wanted. But most of all they gave her a taste of the kind of new life she could lead as a Christian. Their support kept her from returning to the only life she had ever known — the underworld of drugs. They provided her with a family of people who had similar backgrounds and obstacles — a community of people helping each other. She discovered that she had a family because we are all God's children.

(Details taken from a testimonial in the April 2003, Volume 5, Issue 2 edition of *The New Gate*.)

Proper 12 / Pentecost 10 / Ordinary Time 17
Romans 8:26-39

Nothing Can Separate Us

Who will separate us from the love of Christ? Will hardship, or distress, or persecution, or famine, or nakedness, or peril, or sword? As it is written, "For your sake we are being killed all day long; we are accounted as sheep to be slaughtered." No, in all these things we are more than conquerors through him who loved us. For I am convinced that neither death, nor life, nor angels, nor rulers, nor things present, nor things to come, nor powers, nor height, nor depth, nor anything else in all creation, will be able to separate us from the love of God in Christ Jesus our Lord. (vv. 35-39)

On an episode of *The Andy Griffith Show*, Opie brought home his report card showing that his grades were greatly improved. In fact, he had straight *A*'s. Opie's father, Sheriff Andy Taylor, was so proud. He had encouraged Opie to improve his grades and finally he had.

However, the next day at school, Opie's teacher, Miss Crump, called him to her desk. She had discovered that she had accidentally recorded another student's grades on Opie's report card. He didn't make straight *A*'s after all. He knew his father would be disappointed, but he still resolved to tell the truth about the teacher's mistake.

When he got home, Opie immediately began studying in an attempt to actually bring up his grades. Before he even had a chance to tell his father the truth about his grades, Andy exposed a brand new bicycle hidden behind the couch. It was a reward for his son's straight *A*'s. Opie was stunned, and didn't tell Andy about the grade mix-up, and he didn't take the bike outside for a test drive. He simply excused himself to return to his studies.

The next day, Opie tried to tell his father about the mix-up. Before he could say anything, Andy gave him an advance on his allowance and told him to enjoy his bicycle. At dinner that night, he tried once again to tell his father, but Andy went in the kitchen to help Aunt Bee. Opie overheard Andy telling her how proud he was of his son. He had bragged to all his friends around town and wished he could take a picture of Opie and his report card to send to an out-of-town friend.

While in the sheriff's office the next day, Miss Crump stopped in to talk to Andy about the grade mix-up. At last, Andy discovered the truth — not only did Opie not get all *A*'s, but he received an *F* in arithmetic. He went home to talk with Opie. He called to Opie to come down to the living room, but there was no response. Andy went to Opie's room and discovered a note explaining that the boy was running away.

Andy immediately left in the squad car to look for his son. He found Opie walking despondently down a lonely country road. When Andy got out of the car, Opie explained why he was running away. Not knowing that his father already knew, he told his father the truth about his grades. He ran away because he knew he couldn't keep it a secret forever. He had tried to tell his father several times before, but the weight of disappointing his father was too great. He thought the best thing to do was to run away until he had done something that would make his father proud.

Andy knew that he had contributed to Opie's problem by bestowing gifts and bragging about Opie. He looked at Opie, and offered his fatherly sheriff's wisdom. He said, "Opie, I've got something I want to say to you. When I thought you got all *A*'s that was the most important thing in the world to me. And I made it so important that I made it impossible for you to live up to it. You're my son, and I'm proud of you just for that. You just do the best you can. If you'll do that, that's all I'll ever ask of you."

Sounds like what God would say to us when we make mistakes. Nothing can separate us from God's love. "You're my child. I'm proud of you just for that. You just do the best you can. If you'll do that, that's all I'll ever ask of you."

Proper 13 / Pentecost 11 / Ordinary Time 18
Matthew 14:13-21

You Give Them Something To Eat

Jesus said to them, "They need not go away; you give them something to eat." (v. 16)

I led worship for summer youth camp. We had an incredible worship experience on Wednesday night. We had communion, which is always a significant event at camp. We also had a powerful illustration of how God overcame our sin through the cross. I actually constructed a cross in the midst of it. The youth were very moved by the whole experience.

However, I was concerned about the Thursday night worship. It is the last evening and, generally, the most inspirational. But I really felt we had peaked on Wednesday night. As I looked at what our curriculum had planned for Thursday worship, I saw a big let down. It had a video of a skit that we filmed in camp. It was funny but pretty fluffy. And then we were to have a love feast — similar to communion with bread, but no juice. Surely, it would be anticlimatic compared to the previous night's communion. Besides, most of the youth wouldn't even know what a love feast was, let alone experience any meaning.

Because of a conflict, I had to leave Thursday morning. I came back in time to lead the worship that night. I didn't have any time to "fix" the worship service. When I arrived, I realized we probably didn't have enough bread. And what we did have was starting to mold. I tore off chunks of pre-penicillin, which left some funny-looking loaves. This hardly displayed the glory of God in any way.

We started the service and there were more faux pas. But as the love feast was going on, I realized how wrong I was. In the love feast, the bread represented love. The youth first shared bread within their small group of youth that they had been with all week. And then they were directed to share the bread with anyone else in the camp. I had asked them to pick out someone with whom they had struggled to get along. Or someone who reminded them of a difficult relationship back home. The love feast was extremely powerful. The healing that happened with the youth was incredible.

As I reflected on why the love feast was received so well even after communion, it hit me. The youth were feeding each other. They were sharing the love. As opposed to communion where they were simply receiving from a few leaders, all the youth were answering the call to love one another. They were answering Jesus' call when he said, "You give them something to eat."

The youth were actively involved in the ministry and healing that was taking place. No one was doing ministry for them. They were doing it themselves, and a new understanding of the faith was taking place. They were experiencing that faith as being more than just a relationship with God. They discovered it is also a godly relationship with others.

Proper 14 / Pentecost 12 / Ordinary Time 19
Matthew 14:22-33

Little Faith

Jesus immediately reached out his hand and caught him, saying to him, "You of little faith, why did you doubt?" (v. 31)

Once there were two young brothers who had spent all their lives in the city and had never been to the country. Curious, they decided to take a trip into the countryside to see what it was like. As they were walking along, they spied a farmer plowing. They knew nothing of agriculture and were puzzled by what he was doing.

One said to the other, "What is this man doing? He marches back and forth all day. He is destroying a beautiful meadow with long useless ditches."

Of course the one brother had no answer for the other. So, they moved on. Later in the afternoon, they passed by the same field again. Now, the farmer was sowing grains of wheat in the furrows. The inquisitive brother asked, "Now what's he doing? He must be crazy! He's taking perfectly good wheat and throwing it away into those ditches!" He continued, "The country is not for me. These people are senseless. I'm going home."

And with that, he began the journey back to the city. However, the second brother was a bit more curious and not as impulsive. He stayed in the country and continued to keep his eye on the farmer and his field of long ditches.

A few weeks later he saw a wonderful transformation. Fresh green shoots were emerging from the ground and soon they covered the field with an incredible, unimaginable lushness. He quickly wrote to his brother and told him to return to the country. He needed to see the miracle for himself.

Soon his brother returned from the city. He, too, was amazed at the change — astonished at the growth. As the days passed, they saw the green field change once again. Now, all the green was turning into a golden field of tall wheat. At last they understood the reason for the farmer's work.

After the wheat ripened, the farmer came with his scythe and began to cut it down. The brother who had returned from the city couldn't believe it. He exclaimed, "What is this fool doing now? All summer long he worked so hard to grow this beautiful wheat, and now he's destroying it with his own hands! He is a lunatic after all! I've had enough. I'm going back to the city."

But once again his brother had more patience. He stayed in the country and watched the farmer collect the wheat and take it to his granary. He saw how cleverly he separated the chaff and how carefully he stored the rest. He was filled with awe when he realized that by sowing one bag of seed, the farmer had harvested a whole field of grain. Only then did he truly understand that the farmer had a reason for everything he did.

So often we trust what we can see and rely on ourselves when we don't know what we are doing. One brother had little faith in the farmer, and Peter had little faith in Jesus. Both missed opportunities to experience miracles because of their little faith.

Proper 15 / Pentecost 13 / Ordinary Time 20
Matthew 15:(10-20) 21-28

The Power Of Persistence

Then Jesus answered her, "Woman, great is your faith! Let it be done for you as you wish." And her daughter was healed instantly. (v. 28)

Like so many boys, Reggie Swinton grew up wanting to be a professional athlete. His dream was to play wide receiver in the National Football League. So he was excited when he completed his eligibility at Murry State and was invited to join the Jacksonville Jaguars in April 1998. As a non-drafted free agent, he had little chance to make the team, but at least it was a chance.

He participated in the Jacksonville training camp all summer, but was released by the Jaguars before the season began. Figuring his chances to play professionally might be better in Canada, he signed with the Toronto Argonauts of the Canadian Football League in February 1999. His stay in Toronto was short, as he was traded two weeks later to the Winnipeg Blue Bombers where he was cut five months later in August. He then caught on with the Edmonton Eskimos of the CFL in September, but was released a month later.

Undaunted by his drifting, he tried his luck with the NFL again and signed with the Seattle Seahawks in February 2000. He once again went through training camp, but was released by the Seahawks before the season began. About that time NBC and Vince McMahan, who was the "brains" behind the World Wrestling Federation, joined forces to create a new professional football league, the XFL. Swinton signed on with the Las Vegas Outlaws, but they cut him in training camp in April 2001.

After not being wanted by six teams in three different leagues, Swinton decided to give up, and go home to Little Rock, Arkansas.

But with the encouragement of his dad, he decided to give it one more chance. He tried out for the Little Rock Twisters of the Arena Football 2 League. It was a semi-pro indoor league where players were paid so poorly that they held full-time jobs. He was initially cut by the Twisters, but then re-signed after the fourth game.

Swinton excelled with the Twisters and set several franchise records, catching 85 passes for 1,463 yards and 33 touchdowns in just thirteen games. However, it was a world away from the NFL. At the conclusion of the season, Swinton resolved to give up his dream and seek a career that could pay the bills. In August 2001, he enrolled in a car salesman school.

At the same time, the Dallas Cowboys of the NFL needed wide receivers for practice until their regular receivers became healthy. Swinton's offensive coordinator with the Twisters, Ron Calcagni, was visiting the Cowboys training camp and mentioned Swinton as a possibility. After a few phone calls, Swinton was in camp.

Swinton started making plays in practice. Before too long, he was making plays in the preseason games both as a kick returner and as a wide receiver. This time, when the final cut-down day arrived, Swinton had survived, making his first NFL team. He, of all people after all those times being cut, was the Cowboys kickoff returner in the season opener.

In his first NFL game, he took the opening kickoff from the Tampa Bay Buccaneers and raced 77 yards, which set up a Dallas field goal. He had his ups and downs during the season. He returned a punt for a touchdown against the Broncos on Thanksgiving Day. However, Swinton also fumbled twice in Seattle. He later admitted he probably "tried too hard" against the Seahawks since they had cut him a year earlier.

But at the end of the season, Swinton's persistence had paid off. He had established himself as one of the top kick returners in the league. He finished third in the NFL with a 13.4 punt return average and earned All-Pro honors from College and Pro Football Newsweekly. Swinton set four Cowboys records, including combined return yards of 1,741 yards in a season.

The following August Swinton reflected on his journey to the NFL. He commented to DallasCowboys.com staff writer, Nick

Eatman, "I just closed my eyes and prayed to God and thanked him for blessing me and putting me in this situation. He brought me a long, long way."

Persistence based on faith can bring wonderful blessings.

Proper 16 / Pentecost 14 / Ordinary Time 21
Romans 12:1-8

The Ungrateful Mouse

> *For by the grace given to me I say to everyone among you not to think of yourself more highly than you ought to think, but to think with sober judgment, each according to the measure of faith that God has assigned. (v. 3)*

Once upon a time there was a magical old hermit who lived in the forests of India. He spent his time meditating and praying to God. One day the old man was sitting in the forest meditating. A tiny little mouse ran by him when suddenly a big crow came lunging down after the little mouse. The bird's claws were stretched out ready to grab the mouse and gobble him up.

Swiftly the old man jumped up and snatched the tiny mouse out of the bird's claws. He then shooed away the crow. The kind old hermit took the mouse to his little hut in the forest where he gave the mouse rice to eat and milk to drink. He said to the mouse, "Don't worry, little mouse. I will take care of you."

No sooner had he spoken these words than a hungry cat crept toward the hut with his eyes piercing the tiny mouse. So the old hermit used his magic to turn the tiny mouse into a great big cat. Frightened, the smaller cat ran away hungry.

All was fine until that night, when a big mangy mutt lumbered into the forest. When he came upon the cat, a chase ensued. The noise woke the magical hermit. When he saw the snarling mutt, he turned the cat into an even bigger dog. The mutt ran away with his tail between his legs.

Peace was fleeting though. Soon afterward, a hungry tiger came prowling through the forest. The tiger was ready to spring on the dog. Fortunately, the old hermit was praying nearby. With a nod of his head and an incantation, the hermit turned the dog into a larger tiger. The mere shock of it all sent other the tiger away confused.

The tiny mouse had been transformed into a mighty tiger. No one would dare provoke him now. But pride accompanied his transformation. All day long he strutted through the forest. He bragged about how big he was — lording it over all the other animals. He began to order them around as if he ruled the forest.

The hermit noticed the change in the animal. He reprimanded him, saying, "Why are you acting like you are better than everyone else? Remember, you were once just a tiny little mouse. You wouldn't even be alive if I hadn't saved you!"

By this time the tiger was full of himself. He muttered under his breath, "I don't have to listen to this! I'm bigger than that old man. I'll kill him!"

So the next day, as the kind old hermit was sitting and praying, the huge tiger crept up behind him. He crouched into pouncing position. He stuck out the razor-sharp claws on his front paws. And then he quickly and powerfully lunged at the hermit.

But the old man had seen the tiger coming. With a wave of his hand, he changed the mighty tiger back into a tiny mouse. The mouse tumbled helplessly to the ground. The hermit sighed, "You ungrateful creature! You thought you were better than everyone else, but you forgot who made you strong and powerful!"

And with those words, the frightened little mouse ran off into the forest never to be heard from again.

Proper 17 / Pentecost 15 / Ordinary Time 22
Romans 12:9-21

Healing In The Heartland

Do not be overcome by evil, but overcome evil with good. (v. 21)

At 9:02 p.m., July 4, 2001, I sat at the property of Fifth and Harvey in downtown Oklahoma City. Six years, two months, fifteen days, and twelve hours earlier, the Alfred P. Murrah Federal Building had stood there. Now following the tragic bombing, it is the Oklahoma City National Memorial.

I was at the site for a United Methodist youth worship service. Six hundred twenty people had gathered with our group in this unique setting at this unique time to worship God. I sat in the shadow of dusk six feet away from The Reflecting Pool — a shallow pool of gently cascading water. And that's what I did. I reflected. I sat there with memories of the bombing bombarding me.

On the morning of April 19, 1995, I was at my home in Fort Worth, Texas, completing a paper for one of my seminary classes. In less than a month I would graduate from Brite Divinity School at Texas Christian University. In six weeks, I would return home to Oklahoma to take my first preaching assignment. Over the gentle roar of my dot matrix printer, I heard the phone ring. It was my wife, Hadley. She was calling from work, a bank on the west side of town. She was a bit frantic as she passed on the news she heard from customers and co-workers who were trying to confirm with the television in the break room. A government building in Oklahoma City had been bombed. Her excited concern was warranted because her mother worked at a building just north of the state capital. Of course, we soon discovered that it was a federal building and not a state building. We were pleased that we had escaped personal tragedy, but heartbroken over the heinous act. We were dumbfounded to hear that terrorism had struck the calm innocence of the heartland.

As I sat at the Memorial for the youth worship service, I continued to reflect on every connection I had with the bombing. Mental images of the television flashed in my mind. I once again saw bloody people frantically scurrying around. I saw the picture of the fireman carrying the lifeless body of Baylee Almon. I remembered driving by the rubble where the building had stood a little over a month after the destruction. I recalled conversations with friends who had served as chaplains during the days immediately following the explosion. They had told stories of seeing the carnage — both physical and emotional. Only 23 days earlier, Timothy McViegh had been executed for bombing the building. I was at another youth camp that day. We prayed for his soul. In many ways, I was vividly reliving the event that I hadn't really thought about in several years.

The group of 620 worshipers started singing "Shout To The Lord." Somewhere after the words, "My Jesus, my savior," I started to quietly release the emotions associated with the senseless loss of lives. My eyes welled up with sadness expressed with tears. At the same time, I found comfort in singing what I believed — salvation is available through Jesus. It is available to me, to you, and to the 168 victims. In Christ, there is hope even in the midst of a tragedy.

As we concluded the service, Independence Day fireworks began exploding overhead. Some of the youth were disturbed by it. It was frightening to have "bombs bursting in air" at a place where a bomb had been so destructive. But I looked at it differently. I sat and stared at the beautiful colors. Red. Orange. Sparkling white. They shot up so quickly and cascaded down so gently. Grace. It was grace falling down over us as a reminder of freedom. We have the freedom of free will. Some may choose evil, but when the vilest of evil springs forth, others accept the challenge to prove that good conquers evil. We have the free will to choose the good.

As I sat at the Memorial, I saw the good that replaced the evil. I witnessed a living testament of Paul's words in Romans 12:21,

"Do not be overcome with evil, but overcome evil with good." Certainly there were those associated with the bombing who sought the revenge Paul wrote against in the verses before his words of responding to evil by outdoing it with good. I can't fault their anger. It exists as a reality of losing a loved one to an unnatural and deliberate act. The Oklahoma City National Memorial is a reminder to that act and those losses. But more importantly, it is a reminder not of what has happened, but instead, of what can be. No longer was the area of Fifth and Harvey a pile of rubble — a mound of destroyed dreams. No, this is now a new place of new life. It represents how we can respond to the reality of evil with the much-needed reality of good. On that Fourth of July, I saw that good not only in the Memorial. I saw a sign of God's grace gentling cascading on an earthly people who need it. That, my friends, is the Good News. We can overcome evil with God's good grace.

Paying With Love

Owe no one anything, except to love one another; for the one who loves another has fulfilled the law. The commandments, "You shall not commit adultery; You shall not murder; You shall not steal; You shall not covet"; and any other commandment, are summed up in this word, "Love your neighbor as yourself." Love does no wrong to a neighbor; therefore, love is the fulfilling of the law. (vv. 8-10)

A group of women in Stillwater, Oklahoma, operate a resale shop called Elite Repeat. The store carries a variety of items, including clothing, books, toys, and furniture. The store was birthed and incorporated through an unusual process. One of the store managers, Marie Hesser, explained that a group of friends who met regularly for lunch decided to open the shop. Twenty-seven women were involved with forming the business, with five in management positions. Every decision was made by voting — including the name and the downtown location.

In its first year of existence, the store grossed more than $140,000. Not bad for a new business.

However, what is truly amazing is that the Elite Repeat resale shop was not conceived for profit. None of its 65 employees — including the five managers — is paid. After the rent and bills are paid, the rest goes to help two charities — Habitat for Humanity and the Stillwater Community Action Agency. From the first year's profit, about $45,000 went to each of the charities.

Elite's donations have had such an impact that one Habitat house in Stillwater was named the "Elite Repeat House." The cost of the house was close to the $45,000 donated.

The money donated to Stillwater Action was used to repair the roof on a wing of its building, which is used for transitional housing.

Hesser explained the rationale, "Both of them are strong organizations. They have a good thing going and have a good program set up, but they had no cash flow. This gives them a cash flow."

Elite's donations are expected to make up about half of the funding for Habitat's Stillwater affiliate for the fiscal year ending June 30, treasurer Dale Alspach said.

President of the Habitat board in Stillwater, Kathy Dorr remarked, "I was amazed at the success. They've been invaluable to Habitat for Humanity. They're a wonderful group of people."

Dorr realized how successful the business had become when she purchased a pair of pants for her daughter, who lives in Tulsa, only to find out that her daughter had donated the pants a few weeks earlier.

While the success can be credited to dozens of volunteers, Shirley Brassfield who has been a volunteer since the beginning of the project, gives the highest praise to Hesser. She calls Hesser the "guiding force" behind the group. Brassfield says, "She is one of these people that just gives of herself to her community all the way."

Hesser is an example of loving her neighbor as we do ourselves. She lives Christ's law of paying love with love.

(From an article in the 05/12/03 *Daily Oklahoman*.)

Proper 19 / Pentecost 17 / Ordinary Time 24
Matthew 18:21-35

Forgiving Enough

Then Peter came and said to him, "Lord, if another member of the church sins against me, how often should I forgive? As many as seven times?" Jesus said to him, "Not seven times, but, I tell you, seventy-seven times." (vv. 21-22)

Shaling Mei was studying his Bible when he read Matthew 6:14: "If you forgive others their trespasses, your heavenly Father will also forgive you." He really struggled with the idea of forgiveness. It wasn't that he thought forgiveness wasn't a good thing. It's the putting it into practice that's so hard. And the wrong that needed forgiveness wasn't something simple like a child staining the carpet. No, the issue that Shaling was finding hard to forgive was the rape of his three-year-old daughter.

He knew that forgiving the two men was the right thing to do, but how? Every time he tried, he thought of the disgusting tragedy. His precious little girl's innocence was stolen from her. Surely God's call for forgiveness shouldn't be extended to these animals who would violate a toddler. Shaling was torn between his faith and his humanity. His pain and his tears were so great.

But as he reflected on the scripture and allowed it to penetrate his heart, God opened Shaling's eyes to the process of forgiveness. God first forgives us of our failures, and we, in turn, forgive others of theirs. Shaling said, "Forgiveness sees, not the enormity of the deed, but the enormity of the need to be forgiven." Instead of thinking that a sin is too big to be forgiven, we should see monumental sin as needing even more forgiveness.

As if a light bulb appeared over his head, Shaling thought that a parent doesn't keep a dirty child away from the bathtub. No, the dirtier the ragamuffin is, the faster the parent will get her in the bathtub. Then the parent would gently scrub the ragamuffin until she was transformed back into the child the parents know is underneath the dirt. People don't need forgiveness because they're clean, they need forgiveness because of dirty mistakes. The more dirt we have, the more we need forgiveness.

Because of this simple analogy, Shaling was able to begin the process of forgiving the men who raped his daughter. A tear streamed down his cheek as his healing began and his heart was moved beyond anger. For the first time, he was able to pray for God to forgive what he once thought was unforgivable.

(Taken from the November-December 1995 *Upper Room.*)

Proper 20 / Pentecost 18 / Ordinary Time 25
Matthew 20:1-16

Grace For All

> *"I choose to give to this last the same as I give to you. Am I not allowed to do what I choose with what belongs to me? Or are you envious because I am generous? So the last will be first, and the first will be last."* (vv. 14b-16)

A small congregation was comprised specifically of convicts, ex-convicts, and their families. Special arrangements had been made with the department of corrections to release the prisoners for a couple of hours on Sundays and other special days. The church provided a place for released criminals to worship where they wouldn't be judged for their past.

A large well-to-do church in the same city had developed a special relationship with them. This church had adopted the other as a mission by providing them with much needed finances and volunteers. Once a year they had a combined worship service — a Christmas Eve communion and candlelight. At this service, the city's elite would gather side-by-side with some of the city's less respected citizens.

At this service one year, the minister from the large church was serving communion. He noticed that a district judge from his church was kneeling next to a former thief — a man the judge sent to prison after presiding over his trial. It was in prison that the thief had become involved with the church ministering to convicts. Neither man seemed to be aware of the presence and identity of the other.

After the service, the minister spoke with the judge. He said, "You were so deep in prayer, that I'm not sure you noticed who was next to you during communion."

Before the minister could say another word, the judge interjected, "Oh, yes, I knew who was kneeling next to me. I didn't know if anyone else had noticed. But that was why I was deep in prayer. I kept thanking God for grace. What a magnificent mystery it is! What power!"

The minister let the judge's words sink in. He was impressed with the judge's ability to see the former thief as a changed man. The minister said, "Yes, God's grace is so astounding. It certainly was the catalyst that turned this man's life around."

The judge replied, "What you've said is true, but that's not what I meant. I was thinking of myself."

The surprised minister asked, "What do you mean?"

The judge explained, "The man was a thief. His whole life was lived in the underbelly of society. His neighborhood was filled with drug dealers, prostitutes, thieves, and pimps. Once he encountered the gospel, he knew that Christ was offering a life completely different from all that. He needed help. Salvation was his only hope, and he knew it.

"But look at me. Do I know how much I need grace? I started to go to church while I was still in the nursery. I was taught all the Bible stories. I learned the Apostles' Creed and the Lord's Prayer. I went to Harvard Law School, passed the bar, and eventually became a judge. I'm thought of as a philanthropist and well respected in the community.

"Only by the grace of God could I ever admit that in spite of my accomplishments, I am a sinner — no better or no worse than the man I sent to prison. I may have come into the faith before this man did, but the grace that generously forgives his theft, also forgives all my pride and false sense of accomplishment. I'm saved by grace — because I need it just as much as he does. My accomplishments can't earn God's forgiveness."

That's the thing about grace. It's offered to all of us. No matter what we've done — good or bad. Grace brings us to God, puts us right with God, and makes us want to be more like God.

Proper 21 / Pentecost 19 / Ordinary Time 26
Matthew 21:23-32

Walk The Walk

> *"What do you think? A man had two sons; he went to the first and said, 'Son, go and work in the vineyard today.' He answered, 'I will not'; but later he changed his mind and went." (vv. 28-29)*

A soldier was shot and badly wounded in battle during the Civil War. While in a hospital encampment, a chaplain approached the wounded soldier to offer whatever aid he could. He asked the young man if he'd like to hear a few verses from the Bible. The wounded man said, "I'm really very thirsty; I'd rather have some water." The chaplain reached for his canteen and gave the man a drink. After the soldier took a few swallows, he returned the canteen to the chaplain.

The chaplain then repeated his offer to read some scripture verses. The soldier responded, "No, sir, not now — but could you put something under my head?" The chaplain looked around. There weren't any pillows, but he spotted a wool blanket in the corner of the tent. He picked it up and carefully folded it and fluffed it into a makeshift pillow. He very gently placed it under the soldier's head propping him up to give as much comfort as possible.

Once again, the chaplain asked about reading verses from the Bible. "No," said the soldier, "I'm cold. Could you cover me up?" With the extra blanket already being used as a pillow, the chaplain took off his coat and laid it on the soldier, meticulously tucking the soldier in.

Feeling that he had done all he could do for the soldier, the chaplain began to leave without repeating his offer to read scripture. After the chaplain took two steps, the soldier called out to him, "Wait." The chaplain stopped, and slowly turned back toward the soldier. The young man then whispered, "Look, Chaplain, if there's anything in that book of yours that makes you help someone like you've helped me, then I want to hear it."

Proper 22 / Pentecost 20 / Ordinary Time 27
Philippians 3:4b-14

Who's Pressing On?

For his sake I have suffered the loss of all things, and I regard them as rubbish, in order that I may gain Christ and be found in him, not having a righteousness of my own that comes from the law, but one that comes through faith in Christ, the righteousness from God based on faith. I want to know Christ and the power of his resurrection and the sharing of his sufferings by becoming like him in his death, if somehow I may attain the resurrection from the dead. Not that I have already obtained this or have already reached the goal; but I press on to make it my own. (vv. 8b-12)

Distant Friends was an independent Christian rock band who played regionally in Kansas, Oklahoma, and Texas, in the mid 1980s. In July 1988, the band narrowly missed receiving a national recording contract when they played at the Cornerstone Festival near Chicago, Illinois. They disbanded shortly afterward.

One time the band played at a huge amphitheater in El Dorado, Kansas. One hundred or so youth gathered in front of the stage to listen to the band. These youth shouted and cheered. Since it was a Baptist gathering, they did not dance, although, there was some "creative movement" going on. Generally, the youth were having a good time throughout the concert all in the name of Christ.

About 100 feet from the stage was the soundboard that controlled the volume and mix of the different vocals and instruments. It was being run by the band's soundman, Dave, who was a professional sound engineer. Dave was also a sweet, sensitive guy and a sincere Christian. Being involved with music in the 1980s, Dave also had long hair.

Sitting a few rows back from Dave, were a couple of elderly women. Throughout the concert, they kept badgering Dave. They complained that the sound was too loud, although they didn't move to the available seating further back. The women acted childishly as they reverted to name calling. They kept referring to Dave as a "long-haired hippie" as they spoke loudly enough for him to hear but never directly to him.

During the band's concerts, it was their custom for the drummer, Ron Lion, to speak to the youth. He always asked the question, "Is there anyone here who believes that he or she has never sinned?" It was meant to be rhetorical, but there were a few smart aleck kids who raised their hands. When that happened, Ron would humorously reply, "Now we know where the liars are."

Well, when Ron asked the question in El Dorado, these two little old ladies who had been rude to Dave shot their hands up to proclaim that they were without sin. They weren't happy when Ron insinuated they were liars. In fact, they were highly offended.

But it poses a question: Who was pressing on to know Christ? And who was confident of their own accomplishments? Sadly, the little old ladies were the ones who had lost focus in the faith and had forgotten Christ as their goal. But Dave was sharing in Christ's sufferings as he was being persecuted for his appearance. Dave never retaliated with more name calling, but continued to act in a Christ-like way.

Proper 23 / Pentecost 21 / Ordinary Time 28
Philippians 4:1-9

Rejoice?

Rejoice in the Lord always; again I will say, Rejoice." (v. 4)

It was a Tuesday afternoon and the minister began to work on his sermon. He was frustrated and depressed. He was looking at five meetings over the next three evenings — including the evening of his anniversary. He thought, "Ugh! There goes my family time! Again."

That depressing thought led to a flooding of other recent less-than-perfect-ministerial experiences:

Two Sundays before, several people mentioned he had preached his best sermon since he'd been at the church. The following Sunday, attendance was the lowest since he'd been at the church — lower than the Fourth of July or Labor Day weekend. The moral he heard was "preach well and nobody comes."

On Monday, he had gone to visit and take communion to the homebound members of the church. Some of the homebound weren't even home. One was napping and wouldn't see him. Another invited him in but seemed skeptical about his purpose for visiting. He thought, "Why bother?"

Also, the church had asked folks to fill out a survey indicating where they would like to serve in the church. Twenty-seven surveys were returned. Not too bad, for a new idea. But of the 27, one person didn't give his or her name, another didn't check anything, and two were children. There were still another 100 who didn't fill out a survey. The minister wondered if anybody was really interested in serving God!

The church was starting a new Sunday school class for young adults. Letters were mailed inviting folks to take part in the class.

Self-addressed stamped postcards were enclosed with a request to send them back indicating whether or not they were interested in the class. Only one was returned.

The minister mused, "In the midst of these failures and my own frustration, I'm supposed to come up with an inspiring and uplifting sermon — one that preaches the love and grace of God!" He stared at the scripture that he had chosen weeks before: Philippians 4:1-9. Verse 4 seemed to scream at him: "Rejoice in the Lord always." He wondered, "God, how can I rejoice amidst all these failures — let alone help anyone else to rejoice?"

He wallowed in depression for an hour and accomplished nothing. Then God answered his question — which, of course, embarrassed him for complaining. He felt God urging him in his thoughts, "We live with junk every day. Something is always going wrong in life. And yet when we choose to quit whining and change our focus, we see there are a multitude of great things in our life as well. Even in the midst of crud, we can still rejoice. The problem is not a lack of blessings; the problem is that we dwell on the bad and close our eyes to the good."

The minister knew the history behind the scripture. When Paul wrote this letter to the Philippians, he was locked away in prison unable to visit the many churches he had established. He loved the people in Philippi more than any other congregation and would have loved nothing better than to have been with them teaching them the gospel. But did he dwell on his imprisonment? Was he all-consumed by the situation of being kept away from his friends? No. He rejoiced. He kept his mind focused on the blessings of God.

Likewise, Paul told the Philippians to be positive. They were to focus on things that were true, honorable, pure, pleasing, commendable, excellent, and worthy of praise, and we are called to focus on these things as well.

In the midst of the minister's pity party, God not so gently reminded him to redirect his focus to the great things in life that were all around him. God said, "Stop feeling sorry for yourself. You have a loving family, and a wonderful church family who have shown care and concern beyond your expectations. The new after-school program and the new in-depth comprehensive Bible study are off to great starts! I am calling new people to the church. Rejoice and be glad!"

You know, things are rarely as bad as we sometimes make them out to be. When we choose to look at the positive instead of the negative, we discover we really do have cause to rejoice. God has blessed us with things that are pure, honorable, and true.

Yes, things don't always go right, but let's not allow that to prevent us from rejoicing over what does go right — rejoicing over what is true, honorable, pure, pleasing, commendable, excellent, and worthy of praise. Be a realist and look at all the great gifts with which God has blessed you. Rejoice in the Lord always; again I will say, Rejoice.

Proper 24 / Pentecost 22 / Ordinary Time 29
Matthew 22:15-22

Poor God!

Then he said to them, "Give therefore to the emperor the things that are the emperor's, and to God the things that are God's." (v. 21b)

One Sunday morning at St. Matthew United Methodist Church in Midwest City, Oklahoma, a young woman invited the children forward for their "moments with children." After the children sat down, she welcomed them and thanked them for coming. She then pulled out two boxes and a large sack containing various items. One box was marked "God's" and the other was marked "Mine."

As she was teaching them about tithing, she put one t-shirt in God's box and nine in her box. She gave God one CD, and herself nine. God received one box of cereal, and she received nine. And she continued through the rest of the items — giving God one of ten Granola bars, one of ten dimes, one of ten Beanie Babies, and one of ten green apples.

At this point seven-year-old Justin measured up the contents of the two boxes. He commented in a sincerely sympathetic seven-year-old voice, "Poor God!"

It's hard to cover up the Truth when it is that apparent. After the chuckles died down a bit, the young lady challenged each of the children to give God one dime for every dollar he or she received as an allowance.

Without much of a problem, we pay our taxes. Money is withheld and sent in to the IRS. At the end of the year, we file our 1040 and pray for a refund. However, so often, we don't withhold God's ten percent to give to God. We give "to the emperor" because we fear the repercussions. However, we fail to give "to God the things that are God's" even though God has loved us so immensely. Poor God!

Pranky, Cranky Heart

He said to him, " 'You shall love the Lord your God with all your heart, and with all your soul, and with all your mind.' This is the greatest and first commandment. And a second is like it: 'You shall love your neighbor as yourself.' On these two commandments hang all the law and the prophets." (vv. 37-40)

For the final two months of our engagement, my wife moved in with her parents. We went ahead and moved the bulk of her possessions into my house early. One piece of furniture was a gorgeous solid oak antique bed. There was an ornamental piece that stretched across the top of the six-foot-high headboard. It was held in place with wooden pegs. Hadley indicated that the ornamental piece hadn't been used in the past, but she didn't know why.

Two days before our wedding, we found out why. We put the ornamental piece in place. We tested it by shaking the bed. The piece didn't budge so we felt it was secure.

Later that evening, I lay down on the bed while Hadley was packing for our honeymoon. I closed my eyes and clunk — the solid oak ornamental piece knocked me in the forehead, creating a two-inch gash. We called a doctor friend in the church who took me to his office to stitch up the cut.

The next day, our families arrived for the rehearsal to discover the stitched-up scab that looked like a caterpillar on my forehead. That evening at the rehearsal dinner, a deputy sheriff arrived asking for me! It seems a young woman had been assaulted and kidnapped the evening before. Her sister was with her and knocked the assailant in the forehead with a 2 x 4. The police checked the hospital records, and I was a suspect because of my head injury.

Obviously, I didn't do it. I would have remembered assaulting and kidnapping someone, but I was still scared. I was a 25-year-old youth minister and part-time substitute teacher. More than once, I had to gently tell teenaged girls that I was not interested in them romantically. I wondered if some confused young woman was crushed that I would no longer be single: *Fatal Attraction, Part Deux*.

However, the why really didn't matter. What mattered was that I was going to jail the night before my wedding. The sister of the alleged victim accompanied the deputy sheriff, and she identified me as the kidnapper. Just before being handcuffed, the truth was told. The deputy sheriff was pulling a prank as a favor to one of my friends — an usher in the wedding. But before we could all laugh about it — not that I was in the mood — my best man led the brigade to kidnap me and take me to Dallas, which was a four-hour drive. Joining in on the kidnapping was another friend, one of my brothers, my future brother-in-law, and one of his friends.

I couldn't stop them, but I did convince them to change the destination to Tulsa, which was only an hour and a half away. During the trip, my eyes were extremely uncomfortable because my new gas permeable contacts needed to come out. They continued to cause pain until I was returned home at 4:00 a.m.

By 6:00 a.m., my family members, who were staying with me for the wedding, awakened me. They were getting around to go decorate the church. Due to a scheduling conflict, we hadn't been able to decorate the night before. The wedding was scheduled for 2:00 p.m.

Before I left for the church, I got into an argument with my brother who still couldn't understand why I hadn't wanted to be kidnapped. Then while at the church, I got into an argument with my fiancée. It was my first chance to talk to her since I was almost arrested and then kidnapped. I knew she had some foreknowledge of the arrest, but I didn't know the extent of her involvement. It turned out she only found out moments before I did, and she insisted they end the prank before I was jailed, which had been the plan. Pre-wedding jitters are tough enough without having to deal with them on two hours of sleep.

When I parked my car, I hid it three blocks from the church because I didn't want the kids in my youth group to trash it. Eventually, they came to me asking where it was parked. I fibbed and told them it was in the staff parking lot. When they replied that it wasn't, I became a master thespian and screamed, "Ah, man! Someone's pulled another prank on me and hid my car." My best man told them that I had hid it; it would be nearby and they would find it if they kept looking. They found it, of course, and gave it the "Just Married" treatment. They had tied string all the way around it, shoe polished the windows, and tied tin cans behind. There was more shoe polish on the paint and aluminum wheels.

After the wedding, we cleaned the car and left for our honeymoon. We had a great time and came back a day early so we could settle in to our home together as husband and wife. However when we returned home, we discovered that members of my family had trashed my house. Since some of them had stayed with me for the wedding, they had access after we left for the honeymoon. They had put confetti in magazines, in beds, in silverware drawers, and in cupboards. They had also put Vaseline on doorknobs, cellophane on toilets, and shoe polished messages on mirrors. Our first day in our home together as husband and wife was spent cleaning the house.

To recap: I was hit in the head giving me a scabby forehead for my wedding. I was nearly arrested and, then I was actually kidnapped. I almost called off the wedding. Both my car and house were trashed. All this in a week's time. Believe me, I was angry with a lot of people for a long time.

You know, with friends like these, who needs enemies? To be fair, none of the culprits consulted with the others. This was not a grand conspiracy. Any one prank might have been tolerable, but together they were too much.

But all these events beg the question: Is this how we show love to one another? We wouldn't choose our wedding to take place with beatings, kidnappings, arrests, arguments, and vandalism. We wouldn't love ourselves that way. And yet sometimes we treat others very cruelly — often even in the name of love.

Proper 26 / Pentecost 24 / Ordinary Time 31
Matthew 23:1-12

Lessons In Humility

The greatest among you will be your servant. All who exalt themselves will be humbled, and all who humble themselves will be exalted. (vv. 11-12)

In *Daily Guideposts, 2000*, Edward Grinnan recalls the lesson of service and humility that he learned from his mother. The family had an inexpensive set of steak knives when Edward was a child. The handles were made of plastic that was formed to look like wood. One steak knife in the set had a warped handle. The plastic had had a less than pleasant experience with the heating element in the family's dishwasher.

Saturday night was steak night in the Grinnan home. Every Saturday night, the warped steak knife could be found as a part of his mother's place setting. She chose to serve the best to her husband and her children while giving the worst to herself.

Over the years the Grinnan family grew smaller as the children grew up and moved out of the house. But even with extra undamaged steak knives now available, Grinnan's mother still chose the humble warped steak knife for herself. Edward witnessed this as the youngest child. He razzed his mother about it, and she would say she felt sorry for the disfigured knife. She had always had a soft spot for the underdog. She would capture spiders in the home and set them free outside before her husband found them and killed them.

The years passed and all the children left home, including Edward. His mother was all alone now as his father had passed away. He stopped in to visit his mother on a Saturday night. And, yes, even all alone, she was still using the near-antique disfigured steak knife.

Edward thought about the steak knife. Why would his mother continue to use it for decades when there were better knives to use? It had to be something deeper than just habit. He knew his mother was a proud woman. She was not without an ego. She would brag about her family, her children, her independence, and her sharp mind.

As he thought about the steak knife, it occurred to him that it was a symbol of how his mother had worked hard at practicing humility. She saw humility as a spiritual discipline. On Good Friday, she would put a small pebble in her shoe to remind herself of Christ's suffering. In the same way, the old bent-handled steak knife was a weekly reminder of humility. By choosing to use that particular steak knife, she remembered to serve others by placing them ahead of herself. And the imperfect steak knife reminded her of her own imperfections — that she had a reason to be humble.

The promise Jesus gave us is that when we are humble like a servant, he will lift us up with a lasting greatness.

Proper 27 / Pentecost 25 / Ordinary Time 32
Matthew 25:1-13

The Perfect Opportunity

Keep awake therefore, for you know neither the day nor the hour. (v. 13)

During World War II, a lieutenant was accompanying his general on a trip while in the United States. They were traveling aboard a civilian passenger train from their base to a base in another state. After boarding the train, they found their booth, which was already occupied by two other passengers — an attractive young woman and her elderly grandmother. Throughout the trip, the four of them visited easily.

Then at one point, the train entered a long tunnel. The car turned to complete blackness. All four passengers sat silent in total darkness. All of a sudden two distinct sounds were heard. First there was the smooch of a kiss. This was then followed by the loud sound of a slap. Then there was silence again.

As the train continued through the dark tunnel, each of the four passengers was evaluating what had just occurred. The young woman was thinking to herself how glad she was that the young lieutenant had mustered enough courage to kiss her, but she was somewhat disappointed that her grandmother had slapped him for doing it. The general was thinking to himself how proud he was of his young lieutenant for acting on his romanticism and kissing the attractive young woman. If he were twenty years younger, he would have kissed her himself. However, the general was also flabbergasted that the young lady slapped him instead of the lieutenant. Now, the grandmother is astonished to think that the young lieutenant would have the gall to kiss her granddaughter, but she is proud of her granddaughter for slapping him for doing it.

Meanwhile, the young lieutenant is completely satisfied. He is trying to hold back his laughter, for he was prepared to take advantage of the perfect opportunity to kiss an attractive young girl and slap his superior officer all at the same time!

The moral: One must be prepared for the opportunity when it arrives.

Proper 28 / Pentecost 26 / Ordinary 33
Matthew 25:14-30

Investing Talents

"For it is as if a man, going on a journey, summoned his slaves and entrusted his property to them; to one he gave five talents, to another two, to another one, to each according to his ability. Then he went away. The one who had received the five talents went off at once and traded with them, and made five more talents. In the same way, the one who had two talents made two more talents. But the one who had received the one talent went off and dug a hole in the ground and hid his master's money." (vv. 14-18)

In *Through the Back Door of the Church*, Thomas Mallonee tells of Oscar, who was one of those average students whose real passion was extra-curricular activities. He excelled at football and basketball. He also loved to sing. He lived six miles out in the country, and could often be heard singing as he walked home from his after-school practices. The neighbors liked Oscar, and he was a familiar sight on the road home in the evenings. Often they would stop and offer him a ride home.

One of the teachers at school heard about Oscar's singing as he walked home from practice. The teacher asked Oscar to join a barbershop quartet he was forming. The quartet sang at most of the school functions and accepted invitations from outside the school as well, especially the churches.

Between Oscar's singing and athletic prowess, he became a popular member of the community. After he graduated from high school, he married his high school sweetheart, had two boys, and remained active in the community. He even continued to sing in the barbershop quartet.

World War II soon broke out, and Oscar was deferred because he was a father. Still he wanted to serve his country, so he left to be a welder at a shipyard to maintain naval ships. After the war, he returned home to work for a local steel company. He was conscientious and a faithful worker and was promoted rapidly. He was highly respected by his peers.

One of the best things about coming home was that Oscar could begin attending church with his family again. He used his singing talents in the choir. The leadership and teamwork talents he learned on the athletic field, Oscar used in serving on the administrative board, the pastor-parish committee, and the finance committee. And using his popularity, he formed a United Methodist Men's Fellowship. He became the president and chief cook for the breakfasts. During the week, he was always sure to invite the men at the plant as well as the members of his church.

There were five other Methodist churches in the valley where Oscar lived. Feeling that pooling together could strengthen churches, Oscar visited each one of these churches, which eventually led to the formation of a cluster of United Methodist Men that met once a quarter.

Oscar retired from his welding job at the steel company and became ill a short time later. Tests revealed that he had a serious lung problem that probably resulted from his many years as a welder. There was no cure. Oscar could only wait and pray that his condition would improve.

When the United Methodist Men of the valley heard of Oscar's situation, they began to pray. Each came to encourage him. Someone always picked him up to attend the meetings.

Gradually, Oscar began to feel somewhat better. He credits the healing as a return on the investment of his talents — the faith and prayer of his brothers in the United Methodist Men groups. It was as if God was saying, "Well done, good and trustworthy slave."

All Saints' Sunday
Revelation 7:9-17

Heroes And Villains

Then one of the elders addressed me, saying, "Who are these, robed in white, and where have they come from?" I said to him, "Sir, you are the one that knows." Then he said to me, "These are they who have come out of the great ordeal; they have washed their robes and made them white in the blood of the Lamb." (vv. 13-14)

A few years back, the movie *Age of Innocence* was released to critical acclaim. It starred Michelle Pfieffer, Daniel Day-Lewis, and Winona Rider. It was a period piece set in the late 1800s and was marketed as a story of love and romance. It was a commercial art film that already was being labeled an Oscar contender.

Viewer response was lukewarm. Some might suggest this was because of an absence of gratuitous sex and violence. Others would just say the film was depressing. Daniel Day-Lewis' character was engaged to marry Winona Rider's character. Before the marriage, he met his fiancée's cousin portrayed by Michelle Pfieffer. The two fell in love, but would not admit it to each other. Social etiquette of the day would not allow the engagement to be broken. Michelle Pfieffer's character could not steal away her cousin's betrothed. The wedding went on as scheduled, and all three characters lived miserably ever after.

As depressing as this sounds, the real reason viewers failed to connect with the movie was a lack of empathy for the characters. No character was "right" or "good." Perhaps the Michelle Pfieffer and Daniel Day-Lewis characters did the right thing by not following their romantic instincts, but they wallowed around in self-pity to the point of making life wretched for everyone around them. In subsequent meetings, passion was evident between the two characters as was the misery of unenacted lust. The characters were neither good nor bad — only gray. Gray — not a bad emotional description of the film.

In stark contrast is the movie *Star Wars*. In *Star Wars*, the bad guys and the good guys are clear cut. Everyone knows to root for Luke Skywalker, Han Solo, and Princess Leia to defeat Darth Vadar and the Emperor. The lines were clearly drawn. There was good, and there was evil. There was no gray.

This is one reason *Star Wars* was so popular and spawned two sequels and two prequels with more in the making. There are no rumors of *Age of Innocence II: Life Stinks, Live With It* or *Age of Innocence III: Return of the Miserable People*. We like heroes. We like to root for the good guy. This battle of good and evil also helps explain our fascination with the biblical book of Revelation. Here, like *Star Wars*, we find clear distinction between good and evil. It is a battle where only one side will emerge as the victor. You know who to pull for.

Revelation 12:7-12 outlines a key fight. Instead of Luke Skywalker and Darth Vadar, we find the Archangel Michael and a dragon known as The Adversary. The Adversary was the embodiment of an entire universe of evil. He was the leader of an army of demons who opposed God's good purpose for humanity. John describes him in Revelation as a red dragon with seven heads and ten horns. He is an ugly embodiment of the dark side of the force.

And in this corner, is Michael, the patron angel of Israel. He has been involved with angelic battles for Israel before having defeated the patron angel of Persia as well as others. He is the commander of God's cosmic army. He is the good guy. He is the hero.

And thus began a cosmic battle that could only be termed star wars. Humanity was at stake and the winner controls both heaven and earth. John doesn't describe the battle. He only gives the result. Michael wins as The Adversary and his army are cast from heaven. As John wrote his Revelation, the defeated dragon set up shop on planet Earth to cause misery to any available scapegoat. One could imagine, The Adversary was behind the making of the *Age of Innocence*, but John was more concerned with the persecution of Christians for their faith. His message was to hold fast to the faith because The Adversary had already been defeated. The Adversary was powerless and his demise was completed in John's vision as he "was thrown into the lake of fire and sulfur" where his punishment is to be "tormented day and night forever and ever" (20:10).

This battle was fought for the souls of humanity — the multitude clothed in white that survived the great ordeal of Revelation 7:13-17. It was God's grace claiming the saints of all time. God makes Michael the victor over the loser Adversary. The Lamb wins, and the people are saved by his blood. So pull for the victor and celebrate the victory that was won for the saints.

Thanksgiving Day
Deuteronomy 8:7-18

Thanksgiving

For the LORD your God is bringing you into a good land, a land with flowing streams, with springs and underground waters welling up in valleys and hills, a land of wheat and barley, of vines and fig trees and pomegranates, a land of olive trees and honey, a land where you may eat bread without scarcity, where you will lack nothing, a land whose stones are iron and from whose hills you may mine copper. You shall eat your fill and bless the LORD your God for the good land that he has given you. (vv. 7-10)

A stretch of Thanksgiving weeks a few years ago were eventful as well as emotional. In 1995, on the Monday before Thanksgiving, my wife gave birth to our first child, our son, Spencer. After three sleepless nights, we were dismissed from the hospital and allowed to come home on Thanksgiving morning. My family had arrived for the birth celebration and the holiday. The extra 25 people at our house made for a festive homecoming. The fact that my family can cook made the memory of the hospital food that much worse. We rejoiced over the food, and we rejoiced when everyone left.

The next year, in 1996, I had a funeral the day before Thanksgiving. Hadley, Spencer, and I had planned to leave after lunch on Wednesday to see family, but our departure would be delayed until after the funeral. On my way to the funeral dinner, I stopped to drop off our church newsletters to Darlene, a church member who volunteered to fold them. After dropping the newsletter off, I was getting back into my '91 Mazda MX-6, which was a low sitting car. As I tried to lower myself into the bucket seat, pain shot from my lower back into my right leg. I could not bend at the waist. For several years, I had suffered from stress-related back problems and sciatica, but only once before had it been this bad.

Even though I had little trouble walking, I couldn't get back into my car. It was now noon, and I was due at the funeral dinner to lead the prayer. I hobbled back to Darlene's house looking like Quasimodo from *The Hunchback of Notre Dame*. There was no phone at my small country church, so Darlene arranged to send someone to tell them to start the dinner without me. I still hoped somehow to be well enough to conduct the funeral.

Hadley was unavailable, and I needed to get home somehow. A quick call to a church member with a van solved the problem. It was easier for me to step up into his van, than it was to bend down into my car. After I arrived home, another church member, an EMT, came over and stretched my back and leg muscles. He also gave me a mild muscle relaxant. Due to all these kind angels, I was able to make it to the funeral. I moved very gingerly and didn't stand very long, but I made it through the service.

And then in 1997, Thanksgiving was an emotional roller coaster. Hadley was pregnant with our daughter. On Spencer's second birthday, we received a call from our doctor. I knew then it couldn't be a good sign. The doctor never called — only a receptionist. Based on Hadley's blood test, there was a good chance our daughter would be born with Down Syndrome. An amniocentesis was scheduled for after Thanksgiving to let us know more about our daughter.

However, at the last minute, another patient canceled an appointment for the Tuesday before Thanksgiving. We quickly packed our bags and left on a two-hour trip to University Hospital in Oklahoma City. Even with our appointment, we waited for hours for our turn. When we actually began the testing, we opted to start with a level three ultrasound. It was safer than the amniocentesis but not as conclusive. Based on the super ultrasound, there were no signs of Down Syndrome. We could still have the amniocentesis done, but the risk of hurting our daughter through the amniocentesis was greater than the odds that she had Down Syndrome.

Fortunately on April 2, 1998, Hadley gave birth to a very healthy baby girl whom we named Bridget. Even then we had another minor scare as part of the placenta was sent for testing. It was amassed into a glob that looked like a cow's liver. We were elated when those tests came back negative.

I don't know if it was my heightened awareness or what, but during Thanksgiving week of 1998, I was anticipating something major to happen again. After the last three Thanksgivings, I was on the lookout. What could possibly happen after the birth of my son, creaking through a funeral, and a scare with my daughter's health? As it turned out, nothing. Well, almost.

This year it happened the day after Thanksgiving. We were invited to a fish fry at Hadley's step-grandmother's house on the lake. After the holiday fare, we were looking forward to some corn-meal-battered crappie. While we were at the fish fry, the Thanksgiving event I had been looking for happened. It really wasn't an event, though; it was a conversation — a few words spoken to me from a near relative — my wife's stepmother's stepfather's granddaughter's fiancé. (Hey, family is family.) He genuinely said to me one simple phrase: "You have a wonderful family."

That trite phrase shook my world. Those often uttered and simple words caused me to reflect. I had spent my Thanksgiving looking for a major, if not catastrophic, event to occur. I could have better spent my time giving thanks for my beautiful wife and children. If I had examined my previous Thanksgivings a little more closely, I would have seen more clearly that I had plenty of blessings for which to be thankful. God had given something for which I had earnestly prayed — a loving, beautiful, healthy family. That is worthy of thanks. So my Thanksgiving event for 1998 was a realization that God is good and has given everything I truly need. I am blessed even though I am undeserving and slow to give thanks.

Christ The King Sunday / Proper 29 /
Pentecost 27 / Ordinary Time 34
Matthew 25:31-46

If Not Higher

"And the king will answer them, 'Truly I tell you, just as you did it to one of the least of these who are members of my family, you did it to me.' " (v. 40)

There was once a rabbi in a small Jewish village in Russia. Every Friday he disappeared for several hours. Now, in some villages this would cause great alarm. After all, people like to keep tabs on their representative of God. However, in this village, the people were greatly pleased. They boasted that during the time the rabbi was missing he had ascended to heaven to talk with God.

A newcomer arrived in town, and he was highly skeptical that the rabbi was ascending to heaven every Friday during his absence. He was determined to discover where the rabbi went and what he was doing.

So early one Friday morning, the newcomer hid near the rabbi's house. He watched him get out of bed and say his prayers. The rabbi ate a piece of bread and then put on the clothes of a peasant. Then newcomer then watched as the rabbi took an ax and a small cart and headed into the nearby forest. The newcomer followed at a safe distance, making sure he wasn't detected. After going deep enough into the forest so as not to be heard, the rabbi picked out an appropriate tree and proceeded to chop it down. He cut it into sections and then split it into firewood.

The rabbi gathered the wood together and put it in the cart. He journeyed back into the village and proceeded to a shack in the poorest section of the village. The newcomer had not been in the village long, but he recognized the shack as the home of the community's oldest living resident — a widow. The rabbi quietly left her the wood, which was enough for the week. Then the rabbi silently returned to his own house.

After witnessing the gift of the firewood, the newcomer stayed in the village. He was so impressed with the actions of the rabbi that he became a disciple of his teaching. Occasionally, he will hear someone in the village say, "On Friday morning our rabbi ascends all the way to heaven." The new disciple will whisper, "If not higher."